What Is Coworking?

A Look at the Multifaceted Places
Where the Gig Economy Happens
and Workers are Happy
to Find Community

What Is Coworking?

A Look at the Multifaceted Places
Where the Gig Economy Happens
and Workers are Happy
to Find Community

Robert E. McGrath

First Printing: 2018

ISBN 978-1-387-66968-4

Robert E. McGrath
Urbana, Illinois, USA

https://whatiscoworkingthebook.com

Dedication

To the memory of my father. I think he might have appreciated this book.

Table of Contents

Preface

0.1 How I Came to Write the Book

In the last two decades, we have seen accelerating changes in the global economy and an emerging "new way of work." Enabled by technology and driven by contemporary capitalism, the new economy is characterized not only by massive concentration of wealth [12, 1] but an "on-demand" or "gig" economy [2, 11]. Increasing numbers of workers are classified as independent contractors or freelancers, working from contract to contract.

> *Seismic shifts in our economy have moved us further away from the conventional 9-to-5 job—when people worked for a single employer, sometimes for their entire career, and relied on their employer for benefits like health insurance and retirement savings. Instead, as the 2016 Freelancing in America survey finds, a whopping 55 million Americans have joined the independent workforce.* ([4], p. 6)

This may be "the future of work" ([7, 6, 10]), but I worry about *the future of workers*.

As I explored the "new way of working", I learned about coworking spaces, local workplaces where the gig economy happens.

It appears that, coworking spaces are one of the principle places where the "gig economy" happens. In their local coworking space, independent workers find the support and inspiration of a community of peers that cannot be found working alone in a home office or café.

With a background in academic computer science and social science, I was intrigued by these new, technologically enabled workspaces. It seemed to me that these contemporary workspaces did not seem to fit conventional models of work, organizational psychology, or office technology. But coworking spaces and coworkers have received surprisingly little attention in academia.

My interest was further piqued by the development of several such spaces in my relatively small hometown. With a plethora of other workspaces available, why would we want or need a coworking space? Even more interesting, it was obvious that these local spaces were significantly different from each other, and seemed to serve different populations of workers.

As I looked at these diverse workspaces, I wondered what exactly *is* coworking?

As I began to explore the question, I discovered that coworking spaces are designed and organized in many ways, creating substantially different "vibes." Notably, it doesn't seem that the physical space itself or specific attributes of the space are critical, and neither are the spaces necessarily physically different from conventional office spaces or from public spaces such as libraries or coffee shops.

Examining the technical infrastructure, I discovered that digital technology and networks are necessary, but hardly defines coworking. So, coworking is technologically enabled, but it certainly is not technologically driven or determined.

Coworking operations are organized in many ways. There are large, international chains, smaller locally run spaces, and tiny (literally) kitchen-table spaces. Some coworking spaces are noisy, nerf-gun-battling, high-tech play spaces a la Silicon Valley. Some are business incubators full of tech startups, others are filled with writers and artists, and yet others are social enterprises dedicated to local community development.

How can these disparate social spaces all be coworking spaces? What are the essential features they share?

The most important part of the answer turned out to be *community, community, community.*

The secret ingredient that makes coworking different from just renting a desk is the development of a *community* of *independent* workers who work in the space. This community is a replacement for a collegial corporate culture found in a conventional workplace.

Essentially, coworking is an antidote to the social isolation of independent freelance workers. This intervention has been astonishingly successful and deserves serious attention.

For one thing, it is abundantly clear that many *coworkers like coworking*; coworking seems to *make workers happy*. Workers also report other benefits, including increased productivity, creativity, and serendipitous collaboration. Far from being a second choice, many workers find coworking is much more desirable than working in a conventional office

Another intriguing observation is that coworking communities are usually consciously created and maintained by a cadre of professional community leaders, who have developed a growing body of knowledge and practice. These leadership practices seem to be drawn from many sources, including conventional human resources, hospitality industries, community organizing, psychotherapy, and even theater. These leaders and their leadership practices have not, so far as I know, been carefully studied.

Clearly, there is something interesting going on here. In 2014, I began to blog regularly about coworking, which has led to this book.

0.2. Whom Is This Book For?

First, this book is intended to be a source of important questions to be considered by ambitious academic researchers.

Coworking spaces and coworking are an interesting contemporary sociotechnical phenomenon, well worthy of study by social scientists from several disciplines, including anthropology, social psychology, organizational behavior, labor economics, architecture, and even applied computer science. Unfortunately, I have found little academic literature and little interest. For academic researchers, this appears to be a "blue ocean" topic of study.

This book should also be of interest to policy makers, activists, and anyone who is interested in the future of workers and the organization of society. There are many important ideas here and possibly some inspirational lessons as well.

Coworking is quite diverse and can be viewed from many perspectives. Much of what has been said and written about coworking is valuable but limited to a relatively narrow viewpoint. This book attempts to correct this tendency, providing a broad and multifaceted view of coworking. I also raise and try to answer some deep questions that are seldom considered, such as *why* does coworking seem to make workers happy?

I hope that this book will be of interest to coworkers, operators, and especially coworking community leaders, who seek a wider understanding of what coworking is and can be.

0.3. What You Will Find Here

This book offers a broad view of coworking, exploring a number of perspectives. I think this is one of the broadest and most thorough examinations of coworking to date.

I review what has been said and written about coworking and coworkers. I point out connections and relationships to social science research and show where coworking has drawn upon practices from a number of fields to create something new.

I also offer some of my own theories to understanding aspects of coworking. These may suggest directions for future investigation.

There are some key topics and questions to consider:

- **What is the role of technology**? coworking is technologically enabled, but not technologically "determined". The ubiquitous technology is put to use to create a diverse array of communities.
- **How does it work?** How are coworking spaces organized, and how are they sustained? What do people do in a coworking space?
- **How well does it work and why?** Coworkers consistently report that they are highly satisfied with coworking and generally "thrive." What makes coworkers so happy and successful (assuming they really are)?

0.4. What You *Won't* Find Here

I certainly hope that this book offers interesting and useful perspectives for anyone interested in or involved with coworking. However, there are several things that this book might have been but really isn't.

This is not a personal testimony about coworking, and neither is it a how-to guide for operating a coworking space. There are plenty of such available, and I point toward many of them.

Neither is this book a shopping guide or survey of coworking spaces. I do not attempt to rate, rank, or recommend any specific coworking spaces. There are already many such surveys and guides.

0.5. Sources and Methods

There are tens of thousands of coworking spaces around the globe, and I could not possibly sample more than a few. The examples I discuss in this book are interesting and instructive cases, but my sample is not scientific, complete, or necessarily representative.

This book is primarily based on exploration of the Internet and academic literature, as well as brief and certainly unrepresentative personal encounters with individual coworkers and operators. I have visited a very few spaces and attended one large conference (the Global Coworking UnConference 2016 [5]).

This is admittedly a limited and incomplete methodology. This book is not a survey of coworking spaces or coworkers, and it does not present firsthand ethnographic data or interviews with practitioners and community members.

Even so, I have found an overabundance of materials on the Internet sufficient for this and several additional books. (How did we do research before we invented the Internet?) This book has grown out of a critical analysis of these diverse materials, seeking to synthesize some general views.

My sources include

- **Home pages**—Every coworking space has a web presence, which is intended to advertise and recruit members. These materials reveal much about the culture and "vibe" of the workspace and its community and tell us much about the diversity of coworking.
- **Documentation**—Many coworking spaces have extensive blogs and other digital materials that explain everything from philosophy to profiles of coworkers (e.g., WeWork [15], NextSpace [9], Seats2Meet [13]).
- **Anecdotes**—There are many testimonials by coworkers describing their experience and evaluations of coworking.
- **Tutorials**—There is a growing body of how-to guides for coworking community operators and leaders.
- **Trade publications**—There are blogs and digital magazines (e.g., New Worker Magazine [8], Deskmag [3]), as well as coverage in related publications about Freelancing, the sharing economy, digital nomadism, and so on.
- **The coworking movement**—The global coworking movement [14] is an Internet phenomenon styled after open-source projects and internet campaigns.

- **Conferences**—The Global Coworking UnConference meets several times per year, and dozens of regional conferences happen each year.

In addition, there is a small but growing amount of academic literature on coworking, including ethnographic observations and a few surveys.

0.6. Plan of the Book

The book is organized into five sections that examine coworking from different perspectives.

The first chapter introduces coworking with a brief history and definitions and a handful of illustrative examples of contemporary coworking. Chapter 1 concludes with some deep and important questions that will be explored throughout the book.

Part I. Space + Community

The first part considers the fundamental "equation" of coworking:

Coworking = Space + Community

Chapter 2 surveys the common elements and diversity of the physical coworking space, including technical infrastructure and "amenities." Chapter 3 examines the critical social features of coworking, namely the community. This leads to questions of who are coworkers, and what do they do in their coworking space?

Part II. Organization and Leadership

The second part considers the organization and leadership of coworking spaces. Chapter 4 looks at the diversity of business models and organizational strategies used in coworking spaces. Chapter 5 explores the fascinating role of community leaders, who play a crucial role in the success of the community and its workers. These professional community leaders draw on techniques from a number of fields, including human resources and social psychology.

Part III. How Well Does It Work? And Why?

Part III examines what is known about the benefits of coworking for workers and their work.

Chapter 6 looks at provocative research findings that *coworking makes workers happy*. The research also suggests that coworkers thrive and experience improved productivity, creativity, and business networking.

Chapter 7 considers possible explanations for these findings. Are the results to be taken at face value? If so, how well do they extend to other workers and places? Alternatively, are there confounding factors to consider, such as poor sampling, self-selection, or placebo effects?

Chapter 7 also outlines my hypothesis that coworking can be described as a form of "participatory improvised theater": the idea that a coworking space is the stage upon which workers are invited to enact a narrative about "the new way of work."

Part IV. Coworkers of the World, Unite!

Part IV describes the global coworking movement and the evolution of ideas about coworking as a global phenomenon.

Chapter 8 considers the history of the idea of "the coworking movement," and The Coworking Manifesto [14]. In recent years, some have sought to rewrite this narrative, declaring coworking to be a segment of the emerging "service office industry" or as a "platform" for the new economy.

Part V. Conclusion: What Is Coworking?

The last part concludes with a return to the original question, "what is coworking?"

Chapter 9 summarizes what we know about coworking: coworking is all about community, which is what delivers the benefits and attracts workers. The physical space itself is essential as a stage upon which the community is acted out. Chapter 10 wraps up with some speculation on the future of coworking. Coworking can be sustained and will grow but only by diversifying

Chapter References

1. Boushey, Heather, J. Bradford DeLong, and Marshall Steinbaum. 2017. *After Piketty: The Agenda for Economics and Inequality.* Cambridge, MA: Harvard University Press.
2. Chase, Robin. 2015. *Peers, Inc.: How People and Platforms Are Inventing the Collaborative Economy and Reinventing Capitalism.* New York: PublicAffairs.
3. Deskmag. 2016. "Deskmag: The Coworking Magazine", accessed January, 2018. http://www.deskmag.com/
4. Freelancers Union. 2016. Freelancing in America: 2016. New York: Freelancers Union and Upwork https://fu-prod-storage.s3.amazonaws.com/content/None/FreelancinginAmerica2016report.pdf.
5. Global Coworking Unconference Conferences (GCUC) 2018. "Global Coworking Unconference Conferences (GCUC) ", accessed January, 2018. http://gcuc.co/
6. Horowitz, Sara. 2012. *The Freelancer's Bible.* New York: Workman Publishing.
7. Liquid Talent. 2015. "Dude, Where's My Drone: The future of work and what you can do to prepare for it." https://www.dropbox.com/s/405kr9keucv97gw/LiquidTalentFoWEbook.pdf?dl=0 (accessed January, 2018).
8. New Worker Magazine. 2016. About. Accessed January, 2018. http://newworker.co/mag/about/
9. NextSpace. 2016. "NextSpace", accessed January, 2016. http://nextspace.us/
10. Olma, Sebastian. 2012. "The Serendipity Machine: A Disruptive Business Model for Society 3.0." https://www.seats2meet.com/downloads/The_Serendipity_Machine.pdf (accessed January 2018).
11. Oxford International Institute. 2016. "Introducing the iLabour Project", accessed January, 2018. http://ilabour.oii.ox.ac.uk/
12. Piketty, Thomas. 2014. *Capital in the Twenty-First Century.* Translated by Arthur Goldhammer. Cambridge, MA: Harvard University Press.
13. Seats2Meet. 2016. "Seats2Meet - Connecting and empowering you to excel", accessed January, 2018. https://www.seats2meet.com/en
14. The Coworking Wiki. 2015. "Coworking Manifesto (global - for the world) " *The Coworking Wiki.* http://wiki.coworking.org/w/page/35382594/Coworking%20Manifesto%20%28global%20-%20for%20the%20world%29

15. WeWork. 2015. "WeWork: Create Your Life's Work", accessed January, 2018. https://www.wework.com/

Chapter 1: What Is Coworking?

Contemporary coworking is a very interesting sociotechnical development that is not well understood. Coworking has grown rapidly; there are now tens of thousands of workplaces and hundreds of thousands of workers. Coworking is interesting for many reasons.

It is a new way to organize work, or at least it is a novel combination of familiar elements. Coworking builds on ubiquitous office technology and infrastructure, but it does not use conventional office organization. At the same time, coworking recreates important social workplace behaviors in a non-hierarchical, peer-to-peer group.

Coworking is quite diverse. There are many different designs and styles of coworking space, each successful in its own way, and above all else, coworking appears to "work" extremely well: coworkers are happy and productive.

Finally, coworking raises some deep and fundamental questions about work, workspaces, and workers. This book examines these large questions to seek to understand coworking.

This chapter sets that stage with a brief review of the history of contemporary coworking and the basic elements seen in most coworking spaces. The diversity of coworking is illustrated by six example workplaces. The last section poses important questions that will be explored.

1.1. Some History and Background

Like many of the most important cultural phenomena, the origins of coworking are lost in the mists of history—though that history is less than twenty years old, and many of the people in that history are still alive!

It is generally agreed that the contemporary concept of a "coworking space" emerged in San Francisco (where else?) circa 2007 (e.g., [5, 4]). This origin story is disputed (see Brad Neuberg's claim to have invented coworking [17]), and in any case, similar workspaces surely existed earlier, if under different names (e.g., see Deskmag's History [5]).

Regardless of the fiddly historical details, it is pretty clear that the time was right because similar spaces emerged in other cities around the world [5].

What is Coworking?

There may have been many independent inventions of the same idea, coworking may have spread virally across the Internet, or both. In any case, soon there was a global coworking movement modeled after various open-source and Internet-freedom movements. The coworking movement is represented by the *Coworking Manifesto* [30], which declares coworking to be the "future of working." The manifesto was originally promulgated circa 2007 and has been reproduced many times by coworking spaces and coworkers around the world.

Coworking also seems to grow out of economic trends. Ubiquitous Internet technology has accelerated the growth of telecommuting to the point that many workers have become "nomadic," working from wherever is convenient. At the same time, much of the economy has evolved toward the "gig economy," staffed by freelancers and independent contractors [10, 2, 24].

The time was right in another sense: the 2008 crash wiped out many conventional jobs and careers and disillusioned many young workers. Finding no place to go except part-time and short-term "gigs," these workers made a virtue out of a necessity. Many discovered that they would not go back to corporate life and offices were they an option. The crash of 2008 also created a glut of inexpensive office space, which could be used for experiments such as coworking.

As one influential company, Liquid Talent, tells the story, workers wanted to "operate on their own terms and in fun locations" ([15], p. 7). There was a need for a workplace "that combined the energetic, open feel of Starbucks with more collaboration and access to likeminded business types" ([15], pp. 7–8). Enter coworking spaces.

The earliest coworking spaces were inspired by the work environments at famous technology companies like Apple and Google. These corporate offices feature open-plan workspaces, generous amenities, and a freewheeling culture of collaboration and creativity. The social support of a community of coworkers who share similar values, offer mutual help, and have a common identity (similar to a corporate culture) can be a significant contributor to productivity and to organizational and worker satisfaction [1].

Coworking spaces seek to reproduce the best of these attributes without an overarching corporate hierarchy. In a coworking space, independent workers find other workers with similar values and similar job situations who can support each other. This community is a "respite from our isolation" (a la

Klaas [14]) and, as we shall see in later chapters, is an opportunity for increased productivity, creative collaboration, "serendipity" [21], and business networking.

This, then, is the basic picture: coworking spaces developed out of a particular time and place that created a great many independent and freelance workers plying largely digital trades. Both technology and business practices have freed workers from conventional offices but not from the need to be surrounded by colleagues. Coworking offers the benefits of community for these otherwise isolated and homeless workers.

1.2. Example Coworking Spaces

Abstract definitions and descriptions do not really explain the reality of coworking. Another way to understand coworking is to look at examples of coworking spaces and their communities.

In little more than a decade, tens of thousands of coworking spaces have opened (and closed) all over the world (e.g., see directories such as [31, 20]). Many large cities have hundreds of coworking sites and thousands of coworkers. This expansion is marked not just by growth but also by the development of an amazing diversity of spaces and communities of workers. This section describes a handful of coworking spaces. This very small sample indicates the range of physical layouts, organization, and communities found in coworking spaces.

WeWork [35]

WeWork is a chain with sites in dozens of cities around the world. WeWork has tens of thousands of members who can use space at any WeWork site in any city. A WeWork space includes not only office and break areas, but also game rooms, a screening room, and other facilities.

Members of WeWork are generally freelancers and startups, primarily in digital work. The members participate in an extensive digital community, including both work and social interactions and a magazine. WeWork also organizes events for the members, including classes, talks, parties, and a summer camp.

WeWork is similar to many coworking spaces (e.g., NextSpace [18], Impact Hub [11], Grind [7], and Spark Labs [25]). These spaces offer a community with a vibe evoked by the attitude advertised by Strongbox West [26] (Atlanta, Georgia): "Atlanta's largest and most bad-ass coworking space."

Paragraph [23]

It is interesting to contrast Paragraph, which has similar facilities to WeWork but whose members and vibe are quite different.

Paragraph was created by writers for writers, with an understanding that writers work best in a quiet, comfortable space away from the hurry and obligation of urban life.

Paragraph members are writers, not coders or startups. Paragraph, as well as other similar spaces (e.g., theOffice [34] or The Hatchery Press [32]), is designed to be "a quiet place to write," with décor that includes bookcases and books. Events include member readings, agent roundtables, and socials.

Enspiral [22]

Enspiral is a coworking space "for entrepreneurs, startups, freelancers, and charities with an ethical focus"—that is, companies and professionals who are "working together to create a thriving society."

The workspace itself is similar to WeWork and many other coworking spaces, and the workers are software developers and startup businesses. However, the Enspiral workers and companies are committed to their shared social mission, not to purely private profit. There are other similar "social mission" coworking spaces of different scales, such as Make Shift Boston [16] and The Centre for Social Innovation [28, 29].

HeraHub [8]

HeraHub is a chain of coworking spaces facilities and communities that are similar to WeWork, with the addition of features that are designed to attract and serve women professionals.

Hera Hub is the first international spa-inspired coworking space for female entrepreneurs [8].

- Tranquil, yet professional, coworking space designed by and for women
- Numerous networking opportunities with other female entrepreneurs
- Flexible, multilevel memberships
- Supportive workshops and classes

This chain works from the observation that many coworking spaces are dominated by young men and have the vibe of a college fraternity, which is not attractive to professional women. HeraHub has designed décor and the social community to serve "female entrepreneurs."

Reimagination Station [13]

The "reimagination station" is Lori Kane's term for her version of "home coworking" literally in her kitchen. Home coworking is small scale, local, noncommercial, free, and largely self-organized.

Like HeraHub, home coworking aims to serve people in the local community who may not be attracted by the young, White, male membership of other coworking spaces. This and other home coworking (e.g. Hoffice [9] or Jelly [12]) is not a business; it is more of "a friendship incubator," says Kane [13].

The Surf Office [33]

Instead of serving a local community, some coworking spaces focus on the idea that because workers can work anywhere, why not work somewhere really nice? The Surf Office is a "beach villa with coworking space," with locations in Lisbon, Gran Canary Island, and Santa Cruz, California.

The Surf Office and similar locations (such as Nomad House (Bali) [19] and Sundesk [27] (Morocco)) are where "digital nomads come from all over the world to live, work and enjoy the coastal lifestyle." In the same spirit, Coboat offers coworking while cruising the ocean on a sailboat [3].

1.3. What, Then, Is Coworking? And What Should It Be?

Contemporary coworking emerged from a hazy historic milieu and has quickly flowered into a remarkably diverse array of variations on a theme. Nevertheless, it is possible to identify some common features that define the concept *coworking*.

Wikipedia suggests some of the salient features:

> Unlike in a typical office environment, those coworking are usually not employed by the same organization. Coworking is also the social gathering of a group of people who are still working independently, but who share values, and who are interested in the

synergy that can happen from working with people who value working in the same place alongside each other. [36]

A coworking space is an office complex with shared infrastructure, including desks, power, and computer networking. The workspace generally includes some common amenities, including catering, meeting rooms, and rest areas.

A coworking space is also a social environment of likeminded workers who share both infrastructure and, usually, a group culture. The physical space hosts a community whose members network, collaborate, and help each other.

Within this basic template of space + community, there are many, many possible ways to cowork. The chapters that follow will explore the many ways these ubiquitous elements have been and are being combined.

1.4. There Are So Many Good Questions to Ask

Coworking is interesting not just because it is a hot trend, a movement, or a new kind of business. Coworking is of interest to many people besides coworkers, community leaders, and operators. Coworking is a very interesting sociotechnical development a number of academic disciplines, including anthropology, economics, and various social sciences. Coworking is also of interest to policy makers concerned with community development, innovation, the technology of work, the gig economy, and the future of work itself.

Beyond the simple definition and diverse implementation of coworking, coworking spaces and their communities raise questions that lie at the heart of contemporary society and economics. This book seeks to explore these questions and their implications.

This section will set out some of the most important questions,

Causes: The Role of Technology

First of all, coworking is a very important case to study the role of digital technology on work, workers, and how work is organized. There is vast academic literature on this topic and an even vaster ocean of pragmatic and popular thought.

Chapter 1: What is Coworking?

How do contemporary digital technology, mobile devices, ubiquitous networks, social media, and large-scale "platform" computing change the way work can and should be organized? How do workers use and benefit from digital technology? Does digital technology increase productivity and creativity, and if so, how?

Coworking is an interesting example because it is clearly *enabled* by ubiquitous digital and Internet technology. In addition, networks and social media enable digital collaboration and sharing over any geographical distance. Together, these technologies make it possible for workers to "bring your own device" and to effectively work from anywhere. These developments have led to a general rethinking of office work, asking anew, "What is an office for?"

However, despite what is sometimes said, coworking is not technologically *determined*. That is to say, digital technology made possible but did not create or shape the specific forms of workspace that have come to be called coworking.

The evidence for this is very simple and clear. The exact same technical infrastructure and work practices have been folded into many different forms and have been deployed in so many different ways. Digital technology is used in conventional firms and offices, and also by freelancers and home workers. It is also used outside of work in the form of social media, entertainment, advertising, and politics. Digital workplaces, including coworking spaces, are only one of the uses of Internet technology.

For that matter, in coworking spaces themselves, the same ubiquitous digital technology has been and continues to be used in a great variety of ways. As the examples have illustrated, the general idea of coworking has been realized in a great many spaces and by a variety of communities. Digital technology has created a canvas upon which people can paint whatever picture they want.

In fact, there is reason to think that coworking is motivated and shaped by what is *missing* from digital technology. A conventional office not only provides technical infrastructure but also social support, conviviality, and a sense of identity as part of a group of peers and collaborators.

Freelancers and independent workers are immersed in a constantly connected digital world characterized by ubiquitous online collaboration and "community," but many feel a lack of social support from peers and fellow workers. Coworking spaces offer workers a physical, face-to-face community of peers, which cannot be found in the digital world. In a memorable phrase, Zachary Klaas describes coworking as a "respite from our isolation" [14].

In this sense, Coworking in large part is one of many responses to the challenges posed by contemporary digital technology.

Practice: How Does Coworking Really Work?

There are many important questions about how coworking actually works.

Who chooses to cowork, and why? What do people *do* in a coworking space? How are coworking spaces organized; who does what? How are coworking spaces sustained, both economically and socially?

Each coworking space is distinguished from others by its own community culture, enacted by the workers of the community. What kinds of communities have successfully created and sustained coworking spaces? How are coworking communities similar? How do they differ?

One important question is what sustainability or business models work for coworking? For-profit, nonprofit, or not-totally-for-profit? How do coworking spaces recruit and retain members? What kinds of related enterprises and cross revenue sources have been tried? The answers to these questions obviously relate to the nature of the specific community served and its goals.

Coworking communities do not just happen spontaneously. There is a growing cadre of professional coworking community leaders who play a critical role in creating and sustaining the community and help foster worker satisfaction and success. What leadership practices work for coworking and why?

Evaluation: How Well Does Coworking Work?

How well do coworking spaces work? Who benefits, and how? How do people like coworking spaces, and what do they like about them? What are the possible downsides?

There is a growing literature that finds that workers "thrive" in coworking spaces. Coworkers are happy coworking, and report increased productivity and creativity. Can we actually demonstrate creativity or productivity gains? Compared to what?

Assuming that coworkers are, indeed, satisfied and successful, what is it about coworking that contributes to these benefits?

Perhaps coworking is a case of niche marketing, providing a range of workspaces to suit different workers. Unlike a conventional office, dissatisfied coworkers simply depart or never join. This means that the community is, by definition, *self-selected*. Is there a connection between self-selection and worker satisfaction?

Such self-selected communities may easily become demographically homogeneous. Indeed, many observers have commented on the primarily young, pale, and male populations in some coworking spaces. How diverse are coworking communities compared to their local communities?

While the number of coworkers has grown rapidly, not everyone chooses to cowork. Why do workers choose to cowork, and to stop coworking? Are there workers who are poorly served by coworking?

Prospects: Future and Sustainability of Coworking and "The New Way of Work"

What are the long-term prospects for coworking? In part, this depends on the long-term prospects for "the new way of work." Coworking spaces are one of the places that the gig economy happens. Coworkers are primarily freelancers, digital nomads, and solopreneurs—independent workers who work from short-term contract to short-term contract. What are the long-term prospects for these "permanent–temporary" workers? Will digital nomads want to settle down, and if so, when, where, and how will this happen? Even if the freelance workforce continues to grow as some predict [6], will coworking grow along with it?

While coworking overall has grown rapidly, most coworking spaces close within five years (often associated with the expiration of a lease). Most coworkers remain in a particular community for a few years or less. Thus, coworking has seen very high turnover, and the growth of coworking and coworkers has been due to many new spaces and workers entering. Will this continue in the future, or will the pattern change?

Will the birth and death of coworking spaces slow, and will the lifetime of coworking spaces increase? This would mean that coworking communities would tend to become more permanent social organizations, and some of the members would have very long tenure. Such an evolution might lead to a less egalitarian social structure if more established workers claim rights due to seniority.

In recent years, the majority of coworkers have been young, and have coworked for only a few years. In the future, will workers choose to cowork throughout their entire working life? If so, will workers stay in the same community or will workers prefer to switch between communities throughout their career?

How well will coworking spaces serve workers as they age and go through life? Will coworking remain the realm of the young worker, or will it "grow up" as this generation of coworkers ages? The minimal infrastructure and short-term commitment of coworking may match the work life of young workers starting out, but will this formula suit older, more experienced workers? Most coworking spaces do not serve parents of young children very well, and neither are they designed for aging or disabled workers.

Finally, will new business models transform coworking? In recent years there has been an increase in "commodity coworking," provided by large real estate companies. In addition, some conventional companies have sought to create corporate spaces that imitate a coworking space and also have stationed their workers in independent coworking spaces. These developments blur the boundaries of coworking and freelancing, reducing the distinction between "corporate" and "independent" working. This trend also brings potentially large amounts of funding and resources to certain coworking operations, potentially forcing out smaller, niche-oriented workspaces and reducing the overall diversity of options for workers.

Chapter References

1. Allen, Tammy D., Timothy D. Golden, and Kristen M. Shockley. 2015. "How Effective Is Telecommuting? Assessing the Status of Our Scientific Findings." *Psychological Science in the Public Interest* 16 (2):40-68. doi: 10.1177/1529100615593273. http://psi.sagepub.com/content/16/2/40.abstract
2. Chase, Robin. 2015. *Peers, Inc.: How People and Platforms Are Inventing the Collaborative Economy and Reinventing Capitalism.* New York: PublicAffairs.
3. Coboat. 2017. "Coboat", accessed January, 2018. www.coboat.org/
4. De Koven, Bernard. 2013. "The Coworking Connection." *Deep Fun with Bernard De Koven*, August 5. http://www.deepfun.com/the-coworking-connection/
5. Deskmag. 2015. "The History of Coworking", accessed January, 2018. http://www.tiki-toki.com/timeline/entry/156192/The-History-Of-Coworking-Presented-By-Deskmag/#vars!date=1997-05-04_03:19:52!
6. Freelancers Union. 2016. Freelancing in America: 2016. New York: Freelancers Union and Upwork https://fu-prod-storage.s3.amazonaws.com/content/None/FreelancinginAmerica2016report.pdf.
7. Grind. 2016. "Grind Coworking", accessed January, 2018. http://www.grindspaces.com/
8. HeraHub. 2017. "Hera Hub: Workspace for Women", accessed January 2015. http://herahub.com/
9. Hoffice. 2017. "Hoffice: Come and work at someone's home", accessed January, 2018. http://hoffice.nu/en/
10. Horowitz, Sara. 2012. *The Freelancer's Bible*. New York: Workman Publishing.
11. Impact Hub. 2016. "Impact Hub: Experience Collabortion", accessed January 2016. http://www.impacthub.net/
12. Jelly. 2017. "Jelly: Working together is more fun for everyonw!", accessed January, 2018. http://workatjelly.com/
13. Kane, Lori, Tabitha Borchardt, and Bas de Baar. 2015. *Reimagination Stations: Creating a Game-Changing In-Home Coworking Space*: Lori Kane.
14. Klaas, Zachary R. 2014. Coworking & Connectivity in Berlin. University of Illinois at Urbana Champaign https://www.academia.edu/11486279/Coworking_Connectivity.

15. Liquid Talent. 2015. "Dude, Where's My Drone: The future of work and what you can do to prepare for it." https://www.dropbox.com/s/405kr9keucv97gw/LiquidTalentFoWE book.pdf?dl=0 (accessed January, 2018).

16. Make Shift Boston. 2016. "Make Shift Boston", accessed January, 2018. http://makeshiftboston.org/space

17. Neuberg, Brad. 2014. "The Start of Coworking (from the Guy that Started It)." *coding in paradise*, January 16. http://codinginparadise.org/ebooks/html/blog/start_of_coworking.ht ml

18. NextSpace. 2016. "NextSpace", accessed January, 2016. http://nextspace.us/

19. Nomad House. 2018. "Nomad House - Start your online business while exploring some of the most beautiful places", accessed January, 2018. https://nomadhouse.io/

20. OfficeR&D. 2018. "Coworking Directories", accessed January. https://officernd.com/list-of-coworking-directories/

21. Olma, Sebastian. 2012. "The Serendipity Machine: A Disruptive Business Model for Society 3.0." https://www.seats2meet.com/downloads/The_Serendipity_Machine. pdf (accessed January 2018).

22. Our Enspiral Spaces. 2015. "Enspiral Space", accessed January, 2015. https://enspiral.com/our-spaces/

23. Paragraph. 2016. "Paragraph: Workspace for Writers", accessed January, 2018. http://www.paragraphny.com/

24. Piketty, Thomas. 2014. *Capital in the Twenty-First Century*. Translated by Arthur Goldhammer. Cambridge, MA: Harvard University Press.

25. Spark Labs. 2016. "Welcome: Spark Labs", accessed January, 2016. http://www.spark-labs.co/en

26. Strongbox West. 2015. "Strongbox West ", accessed January, 2018. http://www.strongboxwest.com/

27. Sundesk. 2016. "Sundesk: Coworking in Taghazout, Morocco", accessed January, 2016. http://www.sun-desk.com/

28. Surman, Tonya. 2013. "Building Social Entrepreneurship through the Power of Coworking." *Innovations: Technology, Governance, Globalization* 8 (3-4):189-195. doi: 10.1162/INOV_a_00195. http://dx.doi.org/10.1162/INOV_a_00195

29. The Centre for Social Innovation. 2016. "Culture | The Centre for Social Innovation", accessed January, 2018. https://socialinnovation.org/culture/

30. The Coworking Wiki. 2015. "Coworking Manifesto (global - for the world) " *The Coworking Wiki*.

http://wiki.coworking.org/w/page/35382594/Coworking%20Manife
sto%20%28global%20-%20for%20the%20world%29

31. The Coworking Wiki. 2015. "Coworking Space Directory", accessed January, 2018.
   http://wiki.coworking.org/w/page/29303049/Directory

32. The Hatchery Press. 2016. "The Hatchery Press - Where Stories Are Born", accessed January, 2018. http://thehatcherypress.com/

33. The Surf Office. 2015. "The Surf Office Santa Cruz", accessed January, 2018. http://www.thesurfoffice.com/santa-cruz/

34. theOffice. 2016. "theOffice - where creativity takes flight", accessed January, 2018. http://theofficeonline.com/

35. WeWork. 2015. "WeWork: Create Your Life's Work", accessed January, 2018. https://www.wework.com/

36. Wikipedia. 2018. "Coworking", accessed January, 2018.
   https://en.wikipedia.org/wiki/Coworking

Part I. Space + Community

Chapter 2: The Space

A coworking space is a physical space that houses a community of independent workers in the same way that an office is a physical space that houses the workers of an organization. A coworking space provides the infrastructure and functions of a conventional office, usually in space that was designed and zoned for commercial office space.

The first coworking spaces were modeled after Silicon Valley startups: physically simple open-plan work areas equipped with Internet, catering, and play spaces. The idea was to be as open and "fun" as a café but more businesslike. As in the case of large companies and upscale coffee shops, a coworking space may well offer catering, games, and events such as speakers, classes, and parties.

In short, everything that a conventional office has might be provided by a coworking space—with the difference that the workers are "members" (and therefore *customers*), rather than employees.

This chapter examines the features and design of the physical coworking space. The first section sketches the general definition of what a coworking space is and how it resembles other similar workspaces. In fact, coworking spaces are built on the same infrastructure and design principles as other offices and workplaces.

The second section briefly looks at the typical infrastructure to be found in most coworking spaces. This infrastructure is basically a desk with Internet and power (and almost universally, coffee service).

The bare infrastructure is deployed in a space that features an attractive veneer. The third section considers how the design elements and décor of a coworking space helps distinguish it from competitors. Some coworking spaces go beyond office design to distinguish themselves by offering a variety of special features that support both work and work–life balance.

The fourth section will look at some of the ways that coworking spaces are designed to support social interaction, collaboration, and serendipity. The site may include breakrooms, spaces designed for interaction and events, and even direct connections between digital social media and the physical space.

The final section will consider the question of what, if anything, matters about the physical coworking space.

2.1. Key Features of a Coworking Space

First, let's consider some basic questions about a physical space for coworking.

What is special about a coworking space? How does a coworking space differ from other workspaces? What makes an ideal coworking space?

A coworking space is built on the same technical infrastructure as offices and many other spaces, such as coffee shops and home offices. In fact, one reason coworking has succeeded and has expanded so rapidly is that a coworking space does not require special facilities because it uses widely available and inexpensive technology and design.

The design and features of a coworking space are similar to conventional offices, as well as informal workplaces. An independent worker can and often does work in many places, including more than one coworking space. Table 2.1 sketches some similarities and differences among several types of workplaces used by independent workers.

Imagine a coworking space and a coffee shop next door. In both spaces, the people are mostly working on laptops and drinking coffee. In the coffee shop you pay for coffee and sit for free, while in the coworking space next door, you pay for the seat and get the coffee for free.

Table 2.1 Comparison of Coworking and Other Workplaces

Different ways to use office space	Features	Inhabitants
Office	Private space, people work there, plus catering and social interaction.	Workers belong to one organization, which owns and operates the space
Home office	Private space, person works there, plus catering	One worker owns the space, usually only one worker present
Coffee shop, café, etc.	Open to the public, food and beverage for purchase, plus people work there	Workers are independent, do not work for the coffee shop
Coworking Space	Semiprivate space, people work there, plus catering and social interaction	Workers are independent and do not work for the owner of the space

The general template of a coworking space can be, and has been, implemented in many, many ways. The physical space itself might be located in commercial office space, in a refurbished industrial space, in borrowed space in a library or school, or even in someone's home kitchen.

In addition to basic office facilities, each coworking space has its own décor and an array of amenities, such as catering, meeting rooms, lounge, and play areas. Some coworking spaces include more specialized amenities, such as access to a music production facility, gym or spa facilities, childcare facilities, or proximity to a surfing beach.

In short, while coworking spaces are built on ubiquitous technical infrastructure, there is no one right design for a coworking space.

2.2. Infrastructure and Workspace

Coworking spaces have developed out of a broader trend toward digital work. Companies and organizations are reorganizing office work and rethinking "the office" and asking the question, "What does a digital worker really need?"

Digital Infrastructure: Bring Your Own Device

A digital worker with his or her laptop and mobile devices can work anywhere that Wi-Fi is available. Digital platforms such as cloud storage and computation make it possible to access data and computation everywhere. Digital communications like VOIP, messaging, and social media enable effective collaboration with other workers anywhere on the Internet. Table 2.2 lists key pieces of this ubiquitous "bring your own" infrastructure.

Table 2.2 "Bring Your Own" Infrastructure

Early twenty-first IT complex	Provided by
Laptop, one of three operating systems	Worker
And/or mobile device, one of two operating systems	Worker
Wi-Fi or phone	Each site or a public utility
Platforms—social media, VOIP, messaging, content management, etc.	Worker subscribes to public service
The Cloud—on-demand storage, computing (virtual machines), etc.	Worker subscribes to public service

For both workers and companies, the revolutionary innovation is that infrastructure that used to require a large organization to purchase and operate is now available at a low cost everywhere on Earth. (While there are many thousands of coworking spaces on Earth, to date there are none in the rest of the solar system. Yet.) Workers may choose to untether from a fixed office to work at home, at a coffee shop, or to wander the world as a digital nomad. Companies may have open-plan work areas (e.g., [37]), or even no offices at all (e.g., [5]) .

This ubiquitous infrastructure that has enabled "bring your own device" work in many contexts has enabled the creation of coworking spaces. In a sense, a coworking space is an innovative answer to the question, "What do digital workers need?"

On Demand: Desk Space and Other Furniture

In addition to power and a digital network, workers need a place to sit or stand. The most important principle is that independent workers generally don't need a permanent office, which they would use only part of the time.

More specifically, digital workers only need a desk *on demand*, as required by their current work, which might change from day to day. A worker may not need a desk every day, and then he or she may need it around the clock during a busy period. A group of collaborators will need to sit together during the duration of a project, but for the next project they might have a different group of collaborators.

Coworking spaces are designed to support precisely this style of working. A coworking space offers a desk and other facilities on demand, similar to Airbnb, Zipcar, and other on-demand services [7]. It is not surprising that there are many software packages and platforms to implement on-demand reservations and other management services for coworking spaces. These include both commercial (e.g., Cobot [9], LIquidSpace [23], Nexudus [27], or Proximity [35]) and open-source products (e.g., Nadine [29]).

This flexibility is both economically rational (why pay for office space that isn't used?) and satisfies the needs and desires of the workers. A worker may choose not only when but also where and how they want to work at a particular time and pay only for resources they actually use.

Other Features

Coworking spaces may feature a variety of additional amenities that may be added on to the basic infrastructure. These features may distinguish the particular space, attract users, and serve a specific community.

Some spaces accommodate a particular type of work. Some coworking spaces are collocated with lab or shop facilities (e.g., HackerLab (Sacramento) [14] or TheCo (Jackson, TN) [44]). Cohere Bandwidth (Ft. Collins) has a shared practice space for local bands [10], and The Makers Space in Seattle has a Photoshoot Space for professional photography [42].

Other features support the non-work life of the coworkers. For example, one of the most popular amenities is accommodation for dogs and other pets. On the other hand, one of the rarest features is childcare in or near the workspace [48, 21, 49, 24]. Child care is expensive and difficult to provide even for conventional organizations, so it is not surprising that only a few coworking spaces have this service [4, 11, 2, 3, 15].

In a complete combination of work and life, some large cities are seeing the development of "coliving spaces," which offer residential space in the same facility as coworking offices [47].

Coworking spaces also offer "social" amenities that might include not only classes and social events, but also packaged travel (e.g., WeWork's summer camp [46]). These features are similar to those offered by large employers. On the other hand, as noted earlier, some coworking spaces are essentially vacation resorts equipped with Wi-Fi.

2.3. Décor: Setting the Vibe

The basic infrastructure of a coworking space can be packaged and decorated in many ways. Just as a corporate or government office may project a public image of the organization through décor and amenities, a coworking space can evoke emotional and psychological vibes. In the case of a coworking space, though, the image is branding for the community of workers that inhabits the space, rather than their employers.

Even a small sample of coworking spaces illustrates the range of possible designs and vibes, all with a similar core of technology and rental services. Coworking spaces range from giant, corporate complexes, to smaller one-of-a-kind spaces, to borrowed space, leisure sites, and even private homes. Each of these is right for some coworkers and communities.

Some coworking spaces are situated in contemporary buildings, with lots of glass, modern furniture, and highly optimized spaces (e.g., WeWork [46], NextSpace [26], Grind [12], or Spark Labs [39]). Other spaces inhabit refurbished older buildings with exposed structure (e.g., Portland (Me) Engine Room [33], Make Shift Boston [25], Icehouse (New Orleans) [17], [Co][Lab] Urbana [1]). In all these cases, the spaces look very "Silicon Valley," with comfortable lounge spaces and possibly game rooms, exercise equipment, and big-screen TVs.

Some spaces are lavishly decorated and luxuriously comfortable (e.g., theOffice (Santa Monica) [45], Paragraph (in NYC) [31], projective (NYC) [34], Rail Yard (Tucson) [36] or the Hive (Portland, OR) [41]). These spaces may feature handcrafted, bespoke furnishings and professional interior design and industrial chic décor. These spaces are "a design community, designed by a design community" quoting the Rail Yard [36].

Some coworking is hosted within other spaces, such as a public library or school (e.g., Phoenix Public Library [32] and others [19]). Other coworking spaces are embedded in maker spaces and business incubators (e.g., SLO Maker space [38], Women's Business Incubator [48], or Big Bounce in Tempe [6]). In these cases, the space inherits the décor and vibe of the hosting organization.

Some coworking spaces are clearly about lifestyle. There are spaces that offer coworking with surfing, hiking, or other leisure activities (e.g., The Surf Office in Lisbon, Gran Canary Island, and Santa Cruz, CA [43], Nomad House (Bali) [28] and Sundesk (Morocco) [40]). Coboat coworking is a coworking space on an ocean-going sailboat [8].

Finally, coworking can be done in a private home. Home coworking is small scale, done in a kitchen or dining room, with an emphasis on a friendly welcome (e.g. Reimagination Station [20], Hoffice [16] or Jelly [18]). These informal spaces are not designed specifically for coworking, which shows that pretty much any space can be used for coworking.

Soundscape

While much attention is paid to the physical and visual design of coworking spaces, the soundscape is equally if not more important. In any open-plan workspace, workers share a common soundscape, which raises a number of design issues.

One of the primary reasons for coworking is to be among other workers and to be able to talk with them. Personal interaction is an antidote to the loneliness of an independent worker and fosters creativity, productivity, and serendipity. The background noise of other people working and talking contributes to a sense of belonging and being part of a community. On the other hand, ceaseless chatter is not always conducive to work, and there are times when conversation must be private.

A perennial question for coworking spaces is whether there should be music playing aloud, and if so, how loud? What music should play? For some workers, the soundtrack may be a valuable unifying element for the community. For others, it may be an intolerable annoyance.

These challenges are addressed by a combination of technology with group norms and rules. Many coworking spaces have soundproof booths or rooms available for coworkers to use for conversations and phone calls. All contemporary workers, including coworkers, are expected to use headphones, which may be used as a cultural signal regarding readiness for conversation.

Coworking community catalysts Angel Kwiatkowski and Beth Buczynski describe

> [...] universal headphone etiquette:
>
> No ear phones = I'm ready and willing to chat it up, collaborate, brainstorm, or talk about your dog.
>
> One ear phone in = I'm working but also listening to the room, and am in the mood if you want to pass me the link for that funny video.
>
> Both ear phones in = Um, yeah, I'm cracking the human genome over here, please try again later." [19, p. 27]

2.4. Design for Community

Coworking is not merely temporary office space; it is a place for working as part of a community of workers. Later chapters in this book will discuss what kinds of communities develop in coworking spaces and many ways that coworking spaces foster and sustain these communities.

The physical space itself may be designed to enable, enhance, and support collaboration and a feeling of community among the workers. The design may incorporate social spaces similar to those seen in the hospitality industry (e.g., at a convention center or business hotel) such as lounges and break rooms. Larger coworking spaces also have flexible spaces suitable for meetings, classes, and social events.

Many coworking spaces incorporate digital social media into the life of the space. Coworkers generally are digital natives, and many are digital workers, so they have extensive presence and social connections in digital media. Coworking spaces seek to pull this network into the physical space, overlaying the digital community it on a physical, face-to-face community.

In addition to common features such as workplace wikis and chat areas, some coworking spaces aggressively connect digital social media to the community present in the physical space—that is, the physical social network. For example, at WeWork, coworkers create digital profiles that are used for match making and introductions to create and foster in-person collaborations in the physical space [22]. This process is similar to what LinkedIn and other social media do, except it is mapped to the specific people currently present in the space.

Seats2Meet implements an especially elaborate digital augmentation of the physical space, which they term the "virtual blanket" laid over the physical space and people in it [13]. Every worker must provide a digital profile listing their skills, talents, and knowledge, with the agreement that they are willing to share with other workers while in the space. These profiles are projected live on a giant "dashboard", advertising the people and skills available. In this way, Seats2Meet attempts to gain the advantages of digital social networking for the face-to-face network in the physical coworking space.

Seats2Meet views this social networking is valuable enough that they offer both free desk space and buffet meals in exchange for participating in the digital community. They view this as "paying" for your seat with "social capital" [30]. They call this approach "the Serendipity Machine," a digitally augmented physical workplace specifically designed to enable and encourage spontaneous collaboration and networking.

2.5. What, If Anything, Matters About the Space Itself?

Overall, a coworking space is built on ubiquitous, generic digital infrastructure that is identical to what is deployed in conventional offices, cafés, and homes. The desks and office facilities are also similar to those seen in offices, hotels, and business centers, among other locations. This is a rather mundane foundation that is inexpensive and simple to set up and maintain.

On top of this foundation, a coworking space incorporates both add-on features and decorative elements that attract and serve its community of workers. These elements may or may not support the work, but they do act as branding and a context for a local culture and identity for the workers.

A coworking space may be augmented with digital networking and social media, mirroring digital and physical communities in the space. These ubiquitous technologies are used by almost all workers, but using them with a network of real people—people who are present face-to-face—is very significant for the workers and their work.

Looking across the broad range of coworking spaces, it seems clear that there is no one right way to design a coworking space. Does this mean the space does not matter at all?

The physical space is potentially an important symbolic message about the community that works there. Different coworking spaces are known for their own vibes, which are often visible in the physical design. Operators of coworking spaces know that the design of the space may be important for attracting new coworkers, because the first brief impression may determine if she or he joins.

On the other hand, the physical workspace is a sort of theatrical stage upon which the workers enact their play. As in the case of a theater, the stage and props are necessary but hardly the whole play.

In the end, the physical design of a coworking space must suit the community that works there. There are a great variety of possible coworkers and coworking communities, and for this reason alone, there are many right ways to design the space.

Chapter References

1. [Co][Lab]. 2018. "[Co][Lab] Urbana", accessed January, 2018. http://colaburbana.com/
2. Andrus, Aubre. 2015. 7 coworking spaces with childcare designed for better work-life balance. *Mashable*. http://mashable.com/2015/06/13/coworking-spaces-with-childcare/#d7StDjnSyZqm
3. Andrus, Aubre. 2015. "What it takes to set up a successful coworking space with childcare." *Mashable*, July 6. http://mashable.com/2015/06/06/coworking-spaces-childcare/#qbVyas3Vriqz
4. Baug, Kelly. 2014. Having it all: coworking with childcare. *New Worker Magazine*. Accessed January, 2018. http://newworker.co/mag/working-parents-coworking-with-childcare/
5. Berkun, Scott. 2013. *The Year Without Pants: Wordpress.com and the Future of Work*. San Francisco: Jossey-Bass.
6. Big Bounce. 2016. "Big Bounce – Keeping Arizona startups in business", accessed January, 2018. http://www.bigbounce.co/
7. Chase, Robin. 2015. *Peers, Inc.: How People and Platforms Are Inventing the Collaborative Economy and Reinventing Capitalism*. New York: PublicAffairs.
8. Coboat. 2017. "Coboat", accessed January, 2018. www.coboat.org/
9. Cobot. 2016. "Cobot - managing coworking spaces", accessed January, 2018. https://www.cobot.me/
10. Cohere Bandwidth. 2016. "Band Rehearsal Space", accessed January, 2016. https://coherebandwidth.com/
11. Disney, Jo. 2016. "NextKids Closure: Is There a Future for Coworking with Childcare?" *AllWork*, April 22. https://allwork.space/2016/04/nextkids-closure-is-there-a-future-for-coworking-with-childcare/
12. Grind. 2016. "Grind Coworking", accessed January, 2018. http://www.grindspaces.com/
13. Grusauskas, Maria. 2013. The Future of Coworking is Free and Augmented. http://www.shareable.net/blog/the-future-of-coworking-is-free-and-augmented
14. Hacker Lab. 2016. "Startup Coworking Space", accessed January, 2018. http://hackerlab.org/

15. Happy Hubbub. 2017. "Happy Hubbub - coworking with children", accessed January, 2018. https://www.happyhubbub.com.au/
16. Hoffice. 2017. "Hoffice: Come and work at someone's home", accessed January, 2018. http://hoffice.nu/en/
17. Icehouse. 2016. "Icehouse - Leasing office space in New Orleans", accessed January, 2018. http://www.icehousenola.com/
18. Jelly. 2017. "Jelly: Working together is more fun for everyonw!", accessed January, 2018. http://workatjelly.com/
19. Johnson, Cat. 2017. 5 Coworking Spaces and Business Incubators in Libraries That Support Local Workers. *Shareable*. Accessed January, 2018. www.shareable.net/blog/5-coworking-spaces-and-business-incubators-in-libraries-that-support-local-workers
20. Kane, Lori, Tabitha Borchardt, and Bas de Baar. 2015. *Reimagination Stations: Creating a Game-Changing In-Home Coworking Space*: Lori Kane.
21. Kavsen, Rhonda. 2016. "Co-Working Spaces Add a Perk for Parents: Child Care." *New York Times*, December 25, RE5, Style. http://www.nytimes.com/2016/12/23/realestate/co-working-spaces-add-a-perk-for-parents-child-care.html?_r=0.
22. Liquid Talent. 2015. "Dude, Where's My Drone: The future of work and what you can do to prepare for it." https://www.dropbox.com/s/405kr9keucv97gw/LiquidTalentFoWE book.pdf?dl=0 (accessed January, 2018).
23. LiquidSpace. 2017. "The LiquidSpace Network", accessed January, 2018. https://liquidspace.com/network-for-office-space
24. Lodgic Everyday Community. 2018. "Lodgic Everyday Community", accessed January, 2018. https://lodgic.org/
25. Make Shift Boston. 2016. "Make Shift Boston", accessed January, 2018. http://makeshiftboston.org/space
26. NextSpace. 2016. "NextSpace", accessed January, 2016. http://nextspace.us/
27. Nexudus. 2017. "Nexudus: The white-label coworking software", accessed January, 2018. http://coworking.nexudus.com/en
28. Nomad House. 2018. "Nomad House - Start your online business while exploring some of the most beautiful places", accessed January, 2018. https://nomadhouse.io/
29. Office Nomads. 2017. "The Nadine Project", accessed January, 2018. http://nadineproject.org/
30. Olma, Sebastian. 2012. "The Serendipity Machine: A Disruptive Business Model for Society 3.0." https://www.seats2meet.com/downloads/The_Serendipity_Machine. pdf (accessed January 2018).

31. Paragraph. 2016. "Paragraph: Workspace for Writers", accessed January, 2018. http://www.paragraphny.com/
32. Phoenix Public Library. 2016. "About hive", accessed January, 2018. https://www.phoenixpubliclibrary.org/hive/Pages/About-hive.aspx
33. Portland Engine Room. 2016. "Space - Engine room", accessed January, 2018. http://portlandengineroom.com/space/
34. Projective. 2016. "Projective", accessed January, 2018. http://www.projective.co/
35. Proximity Space. 2017. "Connecting Communities & Coworking Spaces", accessed January, 2018. https://proximity.space/
36. Rail Yard. 2016. "Rail Yard", accessed January, 2018. http://www.railyardtucson.com/#the-space
37. Sheridan, Richard. 2013. *Joy, Inc.: How We Built a Workplace People Love*. New York: Penguin.
38. SLO Makerspace. 2016. "Cubicles - SLO Makerspace", accessed January, 2018. http://www.slomakerspace.com/cubicles/
39. Spark Labs. 2016. "Welcome: Spark Labs", accessed January, 2016. http://www.spark-labs.co/en
40. Sundesk. 2016. "Sundesk: Coworking in Taghazout, Morocco", accessed January, 2016. http://www.sun-desk.com/
41. The Left Bank Project. 2016. "Hive at the Left Bank", accessed January, 2018. http://leftbankproject.com/hive/
42. The Makers Space. 2016. "The Makers Space - Seattle", accessed January, 2018. http://www.themakersspace.com/
43. The Surf Office. 2015. "The Surf Office Santa Cruz", accessed January, 2018. http://www.thesurfoffice.com/santa-cruz/
44. TheCo. 2016. "Coworking Maker Space", accessed January, 2018. http://www.attheco.com/
45. theOffice. 2016. "theOffice - where creativity takes flight", accessed January, 2018. http://theofficeonline.com/
46. WeWork. 2015. "WeWork: Create Your Life's Work", accessed January, 2018. https://www.wework.com/
47. Widdicombe, Lizzie. 2016. "Happy together." *The New Yorker*, May 16, 48-55.
48. Women's Business Incubator. 2016. "Women's Business Incubator", accessed March 18, 2016. http://womensincubator.org/
49. Work and Play. 2016. "Work and Play", accessed January, 2018. http://www.workandplaynj.com/

Chapter 3: Community, Community, Community

Temporary office space alone, however it is configured, isn't really coworking. The key ingredient in coworking is the human interactions among the workers in the space. These social interactions instill a feeling of belonging to a *community* of coworkers.

This is really the most important point of this book: coworking is all about community. This chapter introduces some of the main concepts and perspectives, which will be explored in more detail in later chapters.

One of the most important reasons—if not the most important reason—coworking was invented is that independent workers need social interactions with colleagues. A coworking space is designed to provide both the technical infrastructure and *social* infrastructure needed by workers.

Workers find many benefits from joining a coworking community, including conviviality, mutual help, networking, and the serendipity of unplanned collaborations. In short, coworking makes coworkers happy and improves the quality of their work.

Coworkers are drawn from the large and diverse population of independent workers. However, coworking is generally short-term, and a worker may choose to join any coworking community. Coworkers are attracted to coworking spaces that meet their needs and match their preferences, and many workers prefer coworking with likeminded people. This self-selection has led to coworking spaces with relatively homogeneous communities but great diversity across different coworking spaces.

Creating and sustaining community is so important that there are now professionals with titles such as *community manager*. These leaders have developed a pragmatic toolkit for creating and sustaining coworking communities.

Coworking is an international and global phenomenon, too, with thousands of coworking spaces and hundreds of thousands of coworkers, some in almost every city on Earth. Individual coworking spaces have affiliated into larger groupings, and many coworkers identify as part of the global coworking movement.

3.1. Coworking = Space + Community

In the new gig economy, freelance workers, independent contractors, and remote workers can work from anywhere, but one way or another, they need to work *somewhere*. They must find a place to sit or stand with power and Internet. Besides those things, what else do workers need?

Academic studies of telecommuters suggest that one significant drawback of independent working is the lack of social interactions with colleagues (e.g., [1]). In a conventional organization, fellow workers at a common worksite form a natural social network of peers. This social network in the workplace has been shown to be important in two ways: it enhances both the well-being of the workers and the quality of their work.

The presence of coworkers also provides the benefits of conviviality through social interaction and conversation. Workers may also gain a feeling of group identity and have opportunities to practice altruism and mutual assistance. Belonging to a work group motivates workers, helps them overcome stress and difficulty, and is a source of satisfaction.

Independent workers who work alone do not have the natural social environment of a conventional office and often feel isolated and lonely. Contemporary workers are connected and work together via digital media, but this is unsatisfying because "[s]ocial interaction adds a layer of connection to a person that simply cannot exist within a purely digital platform" ([23], p.5). This challenge is certainly not limited to work, many studies have shown the importance and value of face-to-face conversation and community (e.g., see Turkle (2015) [43], Greenfield [12], Kennedy [22], McGonigal [32], Martin [30], or Sheridan [37]).

In short, workers desire and benefit not just from other people being around (which can be found in a café or similar space) but even more from being together in the same physical location with a group of peers who have similar interests. Workers want to belong to a community of coworkers.

Coworking is a direct response to the challenge of providing the physical, technical, and *social* infrastructure needed by independent and remote workers. In the age of digital social networks, a coworking space is a materialization of a social network in a physical space. And the face-to-face community is, as Klaas puts it, a "respite from our isolation" ([23], p. 5).

The importance of community is confirmed by the personal testimony of many coworkers. Workers are inspired and learn from each other:

I found a diverse set of real living, breathing people- resources at my disposal. Watching the way my peers worked, learning how they do business, and seeing them overcome challenges and ignite collaborations opened my eyes to a path of professional development. (From [25], pp. 72–73)

Workers find friendship and emotional support as well:

I am met with smiles and greetings from a diverse and supportive group of people whom I learn from daily and share, collaborate, cry, laugh, and work with. People in the new workforce are not just looking for inexpensive desk rental, they're looking for a sense of belonging, along with professional development opportunities, and fun. (From [20])

Advocates of coworking argue that coworkers gain many tangible and intangible benefits from informal, spontaneous social interactions, including friendship (and perhaps romance [34]), business referrals, enhanced technical skills, and general positive feelings from the spirit of sharing and mutual help (e.g., see Bacigalupo [2], Gradin Franzén and Lindholm [18], Jacobs and Gussekloo [19], Kane [21]), Kwiatkowski and Buczynsk [24, 25], Liquid Talent [26], Marshall [29], Mesku [35], Olma [36], and Surman [39]).

These claims are supported by a handful of studies, such as Spreitzer *et al.* [38], who suggest reasons why people *like* coworking and *thrive* in coworking spaces:

- People who use coworking spaces see their work as meaningful.
- They have more job control.
- They feel part of a community. (summarized from [38])

In short, it is pretty clear that being part of a community is a primary benefit of coworking. Chapter 6 and 7 explore these benefits in more detail.

3.2. Demographics: Who Coworks?

If community is central to coworking, then it is important *who is coworking in the space*. Which workers prefer and succeed in a coworking space? What populations are served by coworking spaces?

First of all, coworking is clearly suited for gig workers, especially those who do digital work. Many types of work are not suited to coworking, per se (for example, retail sales, farming, or transportation), but surveys suggest that there are a large and growing number of independent workers in the gig economy [8-10]. These workers include independent workers—freelancers, independent contractors, remote workers (i.e., employed by but not located at a firm [14]), and even small businesses like "solopreneurs" and startups. This is the primary pool of potential coworkers.

Coworking spaces are favored by digital nomads—workers who have no permanent office (or, in some cases, no permanent home). These contemporary nomads enjoy the freedom to wander the world, working and interacting digitally and taking part in "the sharing economy" [19]. From anecdotal reports, we can infer that this lifestyle is dominated by young, healthy, childless people (and perhaps retired pensioners) [19, 28, 41].

There is relatively little solid information about the ethnic, gender, or cultural make up of coworking communities or of the types of professions represented. Contemporary coworking emerged from a Silicon Valley milieu stereotyped as "digital creatives": young professionals in the software and advertising industries [7]. As in technology companies, this group would be skewed to be young, male, and pale.

This stereotype is reinforced by anecdotes about the unrepresentative and, for some, unwelcoming atmosphere in some coworking spaces. For example, Lori Kane comments on a visit to a coworking space in San Francisco: "[I]t hit me immediately: almost everyone in the space was young and white" (and mostly male). This was "not at all what the walk through the diverse neighborhood primed me to expect" ([21], p. 9).

Another indication that many coworking spaces do not appeal to everyone is the emergence of coworking spaces specifically targeted for women. Felena Hanson captures this view, recalling her impressions from a 2010 visit to The Hive cowoking space in San Diego,

> [W]hile it was a really cool space, with brick walls and concrete floors and dogs running around and ping-pong tables and that type of thing . . . it was a little too cool for me. As a woman, at the time in my late thirties, and having clients that were attorneys and CPAs, it was not quite the perfect spot for me to do business and meet with my clients. [15]

Hanson went on to found HeraHub, a chain of "female-friendly" coworking spaces described as "[t]ranquil, yet professional [. . .]by and for women"

[16]. Women are not necessarily tranquil, of course. The Thrive coworking space offers "a community of like-minded kick-ass women, working, living, and growing together" [42].

Older workers and workers with children are underrepresented in coworking spaces. To date, most coworking spaces have no provisions for childcare. Women's Business Incubator [44] and others are starting to provide facilities and services for parents [4, 31, 27, 13]. This is a significant challenge, and some attempts have had to close [6].

This stereotyped perception of coworkers is not entirely justified. Overall, the ranks of home workers, telecommuters, and freelancers are quite a bit more diverse professionally and demographically and include older people, working mothers, and many ethnicities [9]. A *Deskmag* 2016 survey indicates that a third of coworkers were over 40 years old, 40 percent were female, and about half were married [7].

However, the development of female-friendly and child-friendly sites indicates the principle that different coworking spaces appeal to specific communities. While the overall pool of potential and actual coworkers is fairly diverse, each individual coworking space serves its own community. The result is a diverse universe of coworking spaces, each of which is comparatively homogeneous demographically and ideologically.

Coworkers are free to self-select into whatever community or communities they wish to belong to. Coworkers choose to join a coworking community that attracts them and remain in a community as long as it satisfies them. The 2016 *Deskmag* survey reports that the top reasons to select a specific coworking space are (emphasis added):

1. interaction with others;
2. a community;
3. *like-minded people;*
4. basic office infrastructure; and
5. random discoveries. [7]

In addition to being highly self-segregated, the overall landscape of coworking is extremely fluid. New coworking spaces open all the time, and many close within a few years. Only a few coworking spaces have existed longer than five years. Similarly, coworkers use a given space only part-time and may well work in several different locations during the same period.

The *Deskmag* survey suggests that about two-thirds of coworkers have been resident for three years or less [7].

This continuous churn means that coworking communities are dynamic, with a constant stream of departures and new recruits. This is a challenge for operators (as will be discussed in chapter 5), but it also means that it is difficult to characterize a given coworking community because the membership changes rapidly. For that matter, it should be kept in mind that the demographics of coworking may change quite a bit even in the next few years.

3.3. Leaders Who Excel at Creating and Sustaining Community

Where do these communities come from? How are they created and sustained?

It is widely recognized that this kind of community is not likely to develop spontaneously and may need to be nurtured and helped along. In a conventional office, the workers belong to a hierarchical organization, with leaders and Human Resources offices who help define the culture of the office. The independent workers in a coworking space have no such hierarchical authority, and they must develop their own peer-to-peer community.

One of the interesting developments in contemporary coworking spaces is the emergence of a cadre of professionalized leaders, with job titles such as *community manager, community catalyst*, or *curator*. Whatever the job title, a community leader is responsible for creating and sustaining the community. The leaders work to assure that the workers participate in, find meaning in, and benefit from their coworking community.

To have a successful community, a coworking space must not be a collection of desks where people work; rather, it should be a place where people meet, talk, and come to know each other. Community leaders help bring this about through friendly conversation, personal introductions, and organized social events. The leader also represents the community and its values by telling and living out its story and by teaching new coworkers "how to cowork."

This is not a haphazard or serendipitous process. Many coworking leaders approach community management as a deliberate and pragmatic vocation. As coworking has spread, these coworking leaders have developed a toolkit of practical techniques, which are disseminated though digital media, conferences, books, and training programs. This fascinating new profession and the tools and techniques of coworking leaders are examined in chapter 5.

3.4. The Coworking Movement: A Community of Community Builders?

There are thousands of coworking spaces around the globe, each with its own community of coworkers, each with a local culture. But contemporary coworking is also associated with the idea of a worldwide movement that defines a common identity to these diverse spaces and their workers.

The movement is best defined in *The Coworking Manifesto* [40], a loose statement of "core values" that has been widely endorsed by coworkers and operators of coworking spaces. The movement is also visible in blogs, wikis, and discussion lists, digital publications, and in physical meetings such as the **Global Coworking Unconference Conferences (GCUC)** [11] and many regional meetings. The movement is also apparent in networks and alliances of coworking spaces, which offer workers a worldwide community. Some coworking operators have multiple sites, and coworking spaces band together in local and global alliances.

These links among otherwise disparate workplaces reflect the sense of common purpose among leaders and operators of coworking spaces, who view the coworking movement as *"the community of community builders"* [33]. For workers, the movement offers a flag of group identity and opportunity for a lone, independent worker to be a part of a large and important story.

In recent years, major corporations have moved into the arena with substantial resources to offer large-scale consumer coworking. This has led some to reconsider the coworking movement to be a trade organization, conceived as representing a branch of a larger social office industry (e.g., [5]). This development has drawn a stark contrast between alternative notions of community that lie at the heart of coworking (e.g., [3, 20, 17]).

Chapter 7 examines the coworking movement in more detail.

3.5. Conclusion

By all accounts, coworking is all about community; a coworking space is a *physical location* that is *inhabited by a community of coworkers*. In the new gig economy, independent workers can work from anywhere, and coworking spaces are well suited to their needs.

Independent workers need the social support and collegiality found in conventional organizations. Participating in a coworking community provides both companionship, and improved quality of work through inspiration, mutual help, and collaboration. Chapter 6 will examine the perceived benefits of coworking in more detail.

Most coworkers come from the ranks of independent, freelance, and remote workers—a large and diverse population. However, unlike the workplaces of conventional organizations, coworking communities are self-selected, and workers generally choose to join a convivial group of likeminded workers. The result is that there are a great many coworking spaces, with each community service its own niche and segment of workers.

Contemporary coworking spaces have developed a cadre of professional leaders, with job titles such as community manager or community catalyst. These leaders are responsible for socializing new recruits into the community and for encouraging participation of all workers. Coworking community leaders have developed a toolkit of practical techniques to foster informal conversation, social connections, and group norms. Chapter 4 considers the social organization and business models of coworking spaces, and chapter 5 examines the professional leadership cadres that have developed.

The global coworking movement represents a vision of coworking as a new, ubiquitous, and positive way of work and life. This vision offers otherwise isolated gig workers a part in a larger narrative, as well as connection to their peers around the world. Chapter 7 looks at the global coworking movement.

Chapter References

1. Allen, Tammy D., Timothy D. Golden, and Kristen M. Shockley. 2015. "How Effective Is Telecommuting? Assessing the Status of Our Scientific Findings." *Psychological Science in the Public Interest* 16 (2):40-68. doi: 10.1177/1529100615593273. http://psi.sagepub.com/content/16/2/40.abstract

2. Bacigalupo, Tony. 2015. "No More Sink Full of Mugs." New York: No More Sink Full of Mugs. https://sellfy.com/p/IBtB/ (accessed January, 2018).

3. Bacigalupo, Tony. 2016. "Consumer Coworking." Global Coworking Unconverence, Los Angeles, May 6. http://canada.gcuc.co/wp-content/uploads/2016/presentations/Consumer%20Coworking%20-%20Tony%20Bacigalupo.pdf

4. Baug, Kelly. 2014. Having it all: coworking with childcare. *New Worker Magazine*. Accessed January, 2018. http://newworker.co/mag/working-parents-coworking-with-childcare/

5. Cottle, Frank. 2016. "A Foundation for Change: A single global voicex." Global Coworking Unconference Conference, Los Angeles, May 6. http://canada.gcuc.co/wp-content/uploads/2016/presentations/Foundation%20and%20Giving%20-%20Frank%20Cottle.pdf

6. Disney, Jo. 2016. "NextKids Closure: Is There a Future for Coworking with Childcare?" *AllWork*, April 22. https://allwork.space/2016/04/nextkids-closure-is-there-a-future-for-coworking-with-childcare/

7. Foertsch, Carsten. 2016. "Results of the Global Coworking Survey." Global Coworking Unconference Conference, Los Angeles, May 4. http://canada.gcuc.co/wp-content/uploads/2016/presentations/DESKMAG%20GCUC%20GLOBAL%20COWORKING%20SURVEY%20PRESENTATION%202016%20SLIDES.pdf

8. Freelancers Union. 2015. Freelancing in America: 2015. New York: Freelancers Unioin and Upwork https://fu-web-storage-prod.s3.amazonaws.com/content/filer_public/59/e7/59e70be1-5730-4db8-919f-1d9b5024f939/survey_2015.pdf.

9. Freelancers Union. 2016. Freelancing in America: 2016. New York: Freelancers Union and Upwork https://fu-prod-storage.s3.amazonaws.com/content/None/FreelancinginAmerica2016report.pdf.

10. Freelancers Union, and UpWork. 2017. Freelancing in America: 2017. Freelancers Union https://s3.amazonaws.com/fuwt-prod-storage/content/FreelancingInAmericaReport-2017.pdf.
11. Global Coworking Unconference Conferences (GCUC) 2018. "Global Coworking Unconference Conferences (GCUC) ", accessed January, 2018. http://gcuc.co/
12. Greenfield, Susan. 2015. *Mind Change: How Digital Technologies Are Leaving Their Mark On Our Brains*. New York: Random House.
13. Happy Hubbub. 2017. "Happy Hubbub - coworking with children", accessed January, 2018. https://www.happyhubbub.com.au/
14. Hartmans, Avery. 2016. Here's why Microsoft is giving nearly a third of its New York employees memberships at WeWork. *Business Insider*. http://www.businessinsider.com/microsoft-new-york-workers-wework-2016-11
15. Hera Hub Headquarters. 2015. "Felena's inspiration for launching Hera Hub ". [YouTube Video]. Hera Hub Headquarters, accessed January, 2018. https://youtu.be/OTGP_T-AlQo
16. HeraHub. 2017. "Hera Hub: Workspace for Women", accessed January 2015. http://herahub.com/
17. Hillman, Alex. 2016. The problem with the coworking industry in 2016. *New Worker Magazine*. Accessed January, 2018. http://newworker.co/mag/the-problem-with-the-coworking-industry-in-2016/
18. Hoffice. 2017. "Hoffice: Come and work at someone's home", accessed January, 2018. http://hoffice.nu/en/
19. Jacobs, Esther, and André Gussekloo. 2016. *Digital Nomads: How to Live, Work and Play Around the World*. Amazon.com: Self Published.
20. Johnson, Cat. 2016. Look Out, Coworking. Here Comes Big Money. *Shareable*. Accessed January, 2018. http://www.shareable.net/blog/look-out-coworking-here-comes-big-money
21. Kane, Lori, Tabitha Borchardt, and Bas de Baar. 2015. *Reimagination Stations: Creating a Game-Changing In-Home Coworking Space*: Lori Kane.
22. Kennedy, Pagan. 2016. *Inventology: How We Dream Up Things That Change The World*. Boston: Houghton Miffin Harcourt.
23. Klaas, Zachary R. 2014. Coworking & Connectivity in Berlin. University of Illinois at Urbana Champaign https://www.academia.edu/11486279/Coworking_Connectivity.
24. Kwiatkowski, Angel, and Beth Buczynski. 2011. "Coworking: Building Community as a Space Catalyst." Ft. Collins: Cohere Coworking.

http://coherecommunity.com/shop/coworking-building-community-as-a-space-catalyst (accessed January, 2018).

25. Kwiatkowski, Angel, and Beth Buczynski. 2011. "Coworking: How freelancers escape the coffee shop office and tales of community from independents around the world." Fort Collins: Cohere. http://coherecommunity.com/shop/coworkers (accessed January, 2018).

26. Liquid Talent. 2015. "Dude, Where's My Drone: The future of work and what you can do to prepare for it." https://www.dropbox.com/s/405kr9keucv97gw/LiquidTalentFoWE book.pdf?dl=0 (accessed January, 2018).

27. Lodgic Everyday Community. 2018. "Lodgic Everyday Community", accessed January, 2018. https://lodgic.org/

28. Luthera, Nader. 2016. Coworking our way around the world. *New Worker Magazine*. Accessed January, 2018. http://newworker.co/mag/cowork-the-world/

29. Marshall, Claire. 2015. "How to Make Money (and a whole lot more) by Sharing." Self Published. https://www.sharestories.net/the-book (accessed January, 2018).

30. Martin, Courtney E. 2016. *The New Better Off: Reinventing the American Dream*. Berkeley: Seal Press.

31. McConnon, Aili. 2017. "Starting Up a Business, With Little Ones Close By." *New York Times*, April 20. https://www.nytimes.com/2017/04/19/business/smallbusiness/coworking-spaces-daycare-child-care-entrepreneurs.html.

32. McGonigal, Jane. 2015. *Superbetter: A Revolutionary Approach to Getting Stronger, Happier, Braver, and More Resilient*. New York: Penguin Press.

33. McLaren, Diana. 2015. Australian Coworking Event a Window into Growing Movement. *Shareable*. Accessed January, 2018. http://www.shareable.net/blog/australian-coworking-event-a-window-into-growing-movement

34. Mesku, Melissa. 2015. Coworking: the best place for hookups in 2015? *The New Worker*. Accessed January, 2018. http://newworker.co/mag/coworking-dating-hookup/

35. Mesku, Melissa. 2016. Quantifying serendipity. *New Worker Magazine*. Accessed January, 2018. http://newworker.co/mag/quantifying-serendipity-in-coworking/

36. Olma, Sebastian. 2012. "The Serendipity Machine: A Disruptive Business Model for Society 3.0."

https://www.seats2meet.com/downloads/The_Serendipity_Machine. pdf (accessed January 2018).

37. Sheridan, Richard. 2013. *Joy, Inc.: How We Built a Workplace People Love*. New York: Penguin.

38. Spreitzer, Gretchen, Peter Bacevice, and Lyndon Garrett. 2015. "Why People Thrive in Coworking Spaces." *Harvard Business Review* 93 (8):1-7. https://hbr.org/2015/05/why-people-thrive-in-coworking-spaces

39. Surman, Tonya. 2013. "Building Social Entrepreneurship through the Power of Coworking." *Innovations: Technology, Governance, Globalization* 8 (3-4):189-195. doi: 10.1162/INOV_a_00195. http://dx.doi.org/10.1162/INOV_a_00195

40. The Coworking Wiki. 2015. "Coworking Manifesto (global - for the world) " *The Coworking Wiki*. http://wiki.coworking.org/w/page/35382594/Coworking%20Manife sto%20%28global%20-%20for%20the%20world%29

41. The Surf Office. 2015. "The Surf Office Santa Cruz", accessed January, 2018. http://www.thesurfoffice.com/santa-cruz/

42. Thrive. 2017. "Welcome Home", accessed January, 2018. https://www.thriveaz.com/

43. Turkle, Sherry. 2015. *Reclaiming Conversation: The Power of Talk in a Digital Age*. New York: Penguin Press.

44. Women's Business Incubator. 2016. "Women's Business Incubator", accessed March 18, 2016. http://womensincubator.org/

Part II. Organization and Leadership

Chapter 4: Organization and Operations

How are coworking spaces organized?

A coworking space is a fairly simple enterprise, requiring only generic infrastructure that can be set up in pretty much any location. Even so, a coworking space needs to be funded and managed. In short, a coworking space must operate as some kind of organization.

There are many interesting questions that may be asked. How do coworking spaces operate? What business models are used for coworking spaces? How do coworking spaces resemble other organizations, and how are they distinct?

This chapter examines how coworking spaces are organized and operate.

Given the great diversity of coworking spaces, it is not surprising that there are quite a range of business models and organizational plans in use. Some coworking spaces are nonprofit, some are for-profit, and many are hybrids, combining coworking with other businesses or missions. Coworking is done as a standalone operation, as part of a chain or network, or even in an informal group meeting.

Coworking spaces offer a variety of charging schemes. The core service is short-term desk space, which is often augmented by an array of premium services. In some cases, basic desk space is paid for by the hour or through longer term memberships. In other cases, basic coworking is a loss leader for other services or included with a membership fee. In other cases, coworking is a money-free social exchange.

A coworking space is a shared resource, so there are rules and mechanisms for conflict resolution, though those rules may be fairly minimal. The second section of this chapter examines these governing mechanisms, which may be imposed by the operators of the space or enacted bottom-up by the coworkers. Governance generally reflects the philosophy of the community, incorporating assumptions about the values and goals of the workers. Coworkers generally expect the community to be self-governing, similar to online communities.

The main theme of this chapter is that *there is no one right way to organize and operate a coworking space*. But there is considerable art needed to run a coworking space that sustains a successful and satisfied community of workers. This challenge is met by coworking community leaders, who are employed to manage the coworking community.

4.1. Basic Business Models

How should a coworking space be organized? Should it operate as a for-profit business? As a not-for-profit organization? As some hybrid, or even as part of another business or enterprise? Successful coworking spaces have used any and all of these organizational structures; no one model is best for all spaces and communities.

There is a relatively low bar to creating a coworking business, and this low bar has enabled and encouraged experimentation. As discussed in chapter 2, the physical infrastructure required for a coworking business is ubiquitous and inexpensive. Furthermore, many aspects of operation, such as desk reservation and billing, can be automated. Precisely because it is relatively easy operate a coworking space it is possible to organize it in different ways.

The original concept of coworking was as a not-for-profit, shared resource for the benefit of the workers. In this model, as long as costs are recovered and the workers are happy and successful, a coworking space can be quite successful without significant profit for the organization.

However, sustaining a space generally requires that someone is responsible for the finances. For this reason, coworking spaces are generally organized as businesses, either for-profit or not-for-profit. A coworking space might be organized as a standalone company, as a franchise or branch of a chain, or embedded in another organization. In the latter case, coworking may be subsidized by other business. Each of these approaches has advantages and challenges.

For-Profit Companies

Operating a coworking space is similar to commercial office rental, with many of the same challenges to control costs and maintain occupancy. There are two critical differences between conventional leasing and coworking: the scale or scope of usage and the need to have a social community among the tenants.

In a coworking space, the space typically is rented in much smaller units and for shorter periods of time than conventional office leases. An individual worker may rent a single desk for as little as a few hours at a time. Even if costs and fees are equivalent, a coworking space often receives revenue in small amounts for unpredictable periods of time compared to other rental offices.

Coworkers also desire and expect not just a desk but also a functioning social community. A coworking space needs to create and sustain a community of workers—workers who may leave at any time and can choose other workplaces. This challenge is addressed by professional community managers and an array social events and other amenities. In many ways, coworking resembles a hospitality business like restaurants, hotels, and resorts (not to mention theme parks and cruises).

Just so, some coworking companies have pursued strategies used in the hospitality and other industries, developing large sites and chains of workplaces. Chains such as WeWork [44], NextSpace [27], Seats2Meet [35], and HeraHub [13] provide similar, brand-name services accessible in many locations. This strategy gains economies of scale and standardization. The brand name helps attract members, creates customer loyalty even when they travel, and strives to create a large pool of intermittent workers to smooth out use and revenue.

Similarly, many independent coworking spaces have formed alliances and networks of sites accessible through common "passes" (e.g., Seattle Collaborative Space Alliance [36], League of Extraordinary Coworking Space [41], and CoPass [10]). Key to this approach is a definition of a generic, interchangeable coworking service in the style of a network "platform" for working in the gig economy [19].

This standardization is stretched to its logical limit by Social Office Industry, which promotes "consumer coworking" [20] and rental office space that includes community as "a product" [11]. It is not clear how well this "community as an add on" approach works or whether it should be called "coworking" at all [20, 2]. At the very least, getting the balance right requires thinking about "community first, space second" [22] and attending to the members, not the business, because the members *are* the business [15].

Just as in the hospitality industry, these standardized and large-scale operations sacrifice individual and local character. And just as in the case of restaurant or coffee shop chains, there remains room for independent coworking spaces that offer their own unique, local communities. These two approaches have been described as "authentic coworking" versus "consumer coworking" [20, 2].

Not-for-Profit

The earliest coworking spaces were conceived as shared resources for the benefit of the workers. For example, the *Coworking Manifesto* says that coworking is "[i]nspired by the participatory culture of the open source movement" and describes a set of values that emphasize friendship and collaboration [40]. A coworking space can be quite successful without significant profit for the organization as long as the workers are happy and successful.

There are several variations of nonprofit coworking. The workplace may be formally organized as a not-for-profit entity (or as part of a larger organization), or it may be purely informal, like a club. A not-for-profit organization generally has a formal mission and may be financed in different ways, including membership and user fees. Indeed, there may be little practical difference between the operations of a for-profit or not-for-profit, at least for the workers.

In practice, many coworking spaces operate as "not-just-for-profit" companies [5], formally organized as for-profit companies but operating on the principle of making sure that "if the community is growing and healthy, the business is growing and healthy" [14]. Some spaces may take stakes in a startup in lieu of cash fees or accept sweat equity in the form of work or time donated in exchange for coworking [4].

One advantage of operating as a mission-driven nonprofit is that the mission can match and express the values and goals of a particular community who will use and support the space.

For example, some coworking spaces aim to serve a social mission that is shared among a local community of socially oriented entrepreneurs, artists, or community organizations. The local coworking space may help a community sustain its mission by providing a (physical) clubhouse, providing resources (e.g., Make Shift Boston [24]) or serving as an incubator for social enterprises (such as The Centre for Social Innovation [38, 39]). In turn, the coworking space can benefit from having a ready-made community that shares its mission.

Coworking can also be informal, organized *ad hoc* by the workers. For example, for many years workers have used Jelly to organize "a casual working event" in a local space, such as a coffee shop [18]. These meetings are self-organized and generally free of charge. It is easy to see the similarity between Jelly and, for example, a Meetup [25] or a traditional book club.

Another form of free informal coworking is home coworking (e.g., [6, 16, 21]). This is a "kitchen table" model, in which people open their own home for coworking. The hosts organize the session in their own home, which often includes a shared meal. Lori Kane describes her own concept of home coworking as a "friendship incubator" [21]. Christofer Gradin Franzén and Johline Lindholm developed the "Hoffice" program, organizing local coworking days in people's residences [16]. They explicitly describe this process as "an exchange of gifts."

Hybrid Models Embedded in Other Organizations or Businesses

Many coworking spaces are not necessarily purely for-profit or not-for-profit; they are hybrids with mixed business models. Besides a possible not-just-for-profit philosophy, hybrid coworking operations have two other characteristics: coworking can be added to or embedded in another business, and coworking can offer an array of services.

Coworking is a simple and flexible business that can be incorporated into another business, and a small coworking space can easily be carved out of a larger office or building. This type of relationship generally benefits both the coworking space and the larger organization.

Coworking might be added as a feature within a for-profit enterprise, such as a coffee shop, as well as part of a conventional business center. In this case, the coworking operation adds an extra attraction to the larger enterprise, while also drawing coworkers from the population of the larger organization. For example, Seats2Meet operates coworking spaces in several train stations in the Netherlands, drawing on the vast number of travelers and adding a valuable amenity to the terminal [34]. Another example is The Hive (Portland OR), which is part of The Left Bank Project, a refurbished building hosting two dozen commercial and non-commercial enterprises [42].

Coworking is also offered by many business incubators along with their array of consulting, coaching, and other resources (e.g., Big Bounce in

Tempe [3], Hera Hub [13], SLO Maker space [37], The Center for Social Innovation (Toronto and other cities) [38, 39], and Illinois Research Park [43]). The coworking space offers a low-cost entry point for startups, and the incubator's community attracts coworkers to the space.

Coworking might also be offered within non-profit facilities as a natural extension of the mission for these organizations [12]. For example, some public facilities, such as community colleges or libraries, have coworking space (e.g., Phoenix Public Library [32]). Private non-profits might offer coworking as one of their community services. For example, Enspiral Space (in Wellington, NZ) offers coworking as component of a suite of local community-development enterprises that mutually support each other [31, 26].

Many coworking spaces offer a variety of services besides desk space— some free, some at cost, and some for profit. In this case, coworking might be a loss leader for other business or offered on a menu of premiums. The idea is that inexpensive basic coworking (literally a seat at a shared table) helps to maintain a large pool of workers which promotes the benefits of networking and serendipity, while the premium services provide sustaining revenue.

Premium services generally include meeting rooms, storage, private offices, or custom business services (e.g., legal or accounting services). Coworking spaces host classes and events that may generate revenue.

Finally, a coworking space may ally or cross-promote with other local businesses. These relations can attract members to the coworking space and generate revenue that supports basic coworking. For example, WeWork [44] and other chains offer promotions with local businesses, such as hotels and gyms. Work and Play offers discounted coworking for parents paying for childcare [45]. Some coworking spaces are associated with professional facilities such as shop or studio space, like the Cohere Space, which offers a practice space for bands [8, 9].

4.2. Business Operations: Services, Contracts, and Fees

Operating a coworking space is similar to many other service businesses, with a few unique requirements. The operator owns or leases the space and offers services to customers who are not employees of the space. The customers are the workers who use the space and who participate in the community of workers.

The business operation of a coworking space must answer two basic questions: what services does the coworking operator sell, and what sorts of contracts and fees are commonly used? Different coworking spaces answer these questions in quite a few different ways.

Coworking Services

Operating a coworking space is a pretty simple business. The basic coworking service is on-demand, just-in-time office facilities for individual workers. Coworking aims to provide only what is needed, when it is needed, at an appropriately small charge.

For an individual freelancer or remote worker, "what is needed" starts with a place to sit with power and network connectivity. "When it is needed" is highly variable depending on available work and individual workers' preferences. For most independent workers with sporadic income, it is critical that fees are low and linked to usage.

From the viewpoint of the operator of a coworking space, he or she must the manage office space (building, utilities, furniture, catering) and the community of users (contracts, billing). A coworking operation also deals with marketing the space, community relationships, and organizing events and other extras.

One of the vital functions of a coworking operator is recruiting and retaining workers—that is, attracting and retaining members of the resident coworking community. Criteria for community membership may range from a walk-in, "everybody welcome" policy to a strictly curated, qualified members only policy. In some cases, the community implicitly or explicitly self-selects new members, while in other cases, the operators act as curators who collect specimens to fill out a strategic vision of the desired collection (community).

Marketing is critical for recruiting new members to the space and its community. To do this, the coworking operator creates the public face, which amounts to a description of the space and community. This narrative explicitly or implicitly recounts "who we are" and who should join the community. This includes description of the facilities and amenities, the community vibe (such as "badass," "friendly," "entrepreneurial," or "ethical"), and the benefits of coworking. It is common for a coworking space to cite successful or famous alumni of the space, companies started, or successful projects and products.

In many cases, the coworking operator also puts together a package of benefits for the community. The coworking space may host or sponsor social events, including talks, workshops, and parties. A coworking space may also establish and cross-promote links to local businesses, such as gyms.

Contracts and Fees

Coworking is sold in small units: one seat at a desk, perhaps for as little as a few hours. Like the hospitality and other personal service industries, coworking spaces offer a range of packages and services to attract members and to gain revenue. There is quite a bit of variation in fees and contracts among different coworking spaces.

Coworking spaces offer a range of short-term contracts—monthly, daily, or even hourly—as well as schedules of fees for additional facilities (e.g., a reserved desk, office, meeting room, mail boxes) and access to the community, training, and events.

Some coworking spaces offer free drop-in coworking as space permits, perhaps mixed in with paid members. Seats2Meet takes this free drop-in model to an extreme, offering not only work space but communal buffets for free, charging only for extras such as meeting rooms.

There are a great many possible variations besides direct fees, including taking a stake in a startup in lieu of cash fees, operating like a cooperative, or accepting sweat equity. Informal and home coworking generally operate as a "gift economy," expecting workers to contribute as needed.

It is important to note that many coworking operations believe that their most important feature is the social capital generated by the active participation of the workers. Seat2Meet describes this as "The Serendipity Machine." They do not charge for coworking, but they require workers to participate in the community, thereby magnifying their total social capital and creating "serendipity" for everyone, including paying customers and businesses [30]. Other coworking operations subscribe to similar underlying logic, maintaining low fees in order to maximize participation for the benefit of all.

Many aspects of coworking operations have become rather standardized, partly due to the availability of products to automate these practices. There are many software packages that implement on-demand reservations and other management services for coworking spaces, both commercial (e.g., Cobot [6], LIquidSpace [23], Nexudus [28], or Proximity [33]) and open source (e.g., Nadine [29]).

An illustration of what might be done can be seen in the Cobot management software [6], which automates many aspects of operating a coworking space, including memberships, fees, and other aspects of user management. Their instructions explain how to set up and customize a variety of plans, including monthly or quarterly contracts, short-term "time passes" (e.g., a two-hour pass, a one-day pass), and provisions for "extras" (such as key access) [7].

4.3. Governance and Community Management

In addition to financials and facilities, a coworking operator must manage the community of workers who inhabit the space. One part of this task is similar to many other shared workplaces, including rules and norms and processes for enforcement and conflict resolution. A second aspect of this task is akin to the role of many corporate Human Resources offices, which often are tasked with promoting a healthy work environment, workers' career development, and interpersonal relations.

A key part of the art of operating a coworking space is finding the right rules and processes for the current community of coworkers. Like a hospitality business such as a spa or country club, a coworking business must attract and retain a community of coworkers who are their customers, not employees. In addition, the specific rules and processes are an important part of the distinctive culture of the coworking community and an expression of the group's values.

A coworking operation must resolve many basic questions, such as what sorts of rules are used in coworking communities? Where do the rules come from? How are rules enforced and disputes managed?

There seems to be broad consensus that coworking communities should be largely self-governing, reflecting the preference of independent workers for autonomy. In addition, coworking spaces have seen the emergence of a cadre of professional community managers. These leaders are employed by the coworking operation but work for the benefit of the workers and the community.

Governance

Any workplace needs at least some governance—that is, rules and processes. Coworking spaces face an array of common problems that are similar to those in conventional offices and shared spaces, such as fair use of common resources and resolution of conflicts. For example, the coworking operation needs to regulate access to the space, moderate the general conduct of the workers, and resolve problems that may arise.

In a conventional office, the employer operates the workplace and has the responsibility and authority to govern the workers (employees) there. In contrast, a coworking operator has considerably less authority over the workers. Coworkers are independent workers who do not work for the coworking operator, and they are customers who may leave at any time. In addition, coworkers generally value autonomy, and each local coworking community has its own culture that must be respected.

In general, coworking communities are comparatively self-governing, not unlike digital communities. Indeed, coworkers are generally digital natives and often use social media and digital tools to organize and connect the coworking community. Historically, early coworking spaces were inspired by open-source software development, which employed self-governing, distributed digital communities [40, 17, 30, 22].

In practice, the rules for most coworking spaces usually amount to some form of "don't be a bad coworker." The definition of this commandment is often left to the workers themselves.

A an example, influential coworking advocate Tony Bacigalupo offers his own eight rules in his book titled *No More Sink Full of Mugs* [1]:

1. "Treat people like human beings.
2. Value relationships over transactions.
3. Make everything visibly and obviously accessible.
4. Empower people to handle things themselves wherever possible.
5. Trust by default.
6. Remind people to use their conscience.
7. Practice relentless positivity.
8. Avoid hard rules." ([1], Chapter 1)

There are, of course, many variations on the rules and norms for coworking communities, but Bacigalupo captures the spirit of a self-governing group of peers.

Community Management

It is critical for a coworking business to create and sustain a community of workers. This is a requirement that goes beyond mere occupancy that drives conventional facility management. The workers need to be happy and interacting with each other in positive and productive ways. In this, coworking is similar to the hospitality industry, such as clubs, spas, and resorts.

This sort of community doesn't just happen; it usually takes conscious effort. In practice, community leaders such as Bacigalupo play a critical role in creating and sustaining the community. As Angel Kwiatkowski and Beth Buczynsk put it,

> "*[J]ust finding a room with desks and internet won't cut it. Someone* must *step forward to create and hold the space where productive work and a saturated sense of community can happen at any time.*" ([22], p. 12)

Most coworking operations employ professional community leaders, who are called *community managers, community wranglers, community catalysts*, and a variety of other titles.

These leaders have developed a toolkit of pragmatic methods that go far beyond checking workers in and collecting fees. Community management includes many elements that are the realm of corporate Human Resources departments, such as introducing new workers and maintaining group norms and rules, and providing conviviality and friendly conversation. A community manager also may be concerned with worker career development, promoting a healthy work environment, and problem resolution. Finally, community managers may promote serendipity by promoting collaboration and skill sharing among the workers.

The community manager role is a distinctive characteristic of coworking, and chapter 5 examines these leaders and their tools.

4.4. Conclusion: No One Right Way, but Many Common Practices

The central theme of this chapter has been that there is no one right way to operate a coworking space. The concept of coworking can and has been realized in many different ways.

Successful coworking spaces have been organized in many ways: as for-profit companies, as not-for-profit organizations, and as hybrids. Some spaces are small, local operations; others are large chains with sites in many cities. A coworking space may be part of another enterprise, or it may even be an informal get-together in someone's kitchen.

Nevertheless, there are quite a few common practices that are found in many coworking operations. There is a basic core of services, as well as a variety of widely offered premium services. The array of services is seen by some as a standardized "platform" for coworking, offering commodity services available through digital tools [19].

Governance of coworking spaces is generally much more decentralized, bottom-up, and community-oriented than conventional office spaces. In one sense, this is necessary and inevitable because coworkers are independent and autonomous, and they are customers rather than employees. But this approach is also inspired by Internet culture. The *Coworking Manifesto* [40] articulates the values of openness, collaboration, and sharing, which are explicitly drawn from the norms of social media platforms and open-source development communities.

This is the age of Facebook, the age of the personal network and personalized digital communities. For many workers, a coworking space is a materialization of a digital social network in a physical space, with similar norms and expectations. Just as on social media, workers expect to select their own tribe of coworkers and an optimal office culture.

Also following the lead of decentralized Internet communities, coworking communities have developed a cohort of professional community leaders. These community managers work for the coworking operation and use a toolkit of pragmatic methods for creating and fostering coworking communities. Chapter 5 examines these leaders and their tools.

Chapter References

1. Bacigalupo, Tony. 2015. "No More Sink Full of Mugs." New York: No More Sink Full of Mugs. https://sellfy.com/p/IBtB/ (accessed January, 2018).

2. Bacigalupo, Tony. 2016. "Consumer Coworking." Global Coworking Unconverence, Los Angeles, May 6. http://canada.gcuc.co/wp-content/uploads/2016/presentations/Consumer%20Coworking%20-%20Tony%20Bacigalupo.pdf

3. Big Bounce. 2016. "Big Bounce – Keeping Arizona startups in business", accessed January, 2018. http://www.bigbounce.co/

4. BlogFabrik. 2016. "Blogfabrik - Empowering Content Creators", accessed January, 2018. http://blogfabrik.de/en/

5. Buczynski, Beth. 2011. Coworking as a Business: Which Model Is Best? *Sharable*. Accessed January, 2018. http://www.shareable.net/blog/coworking-as-a-business-which-model-is-best

6. Cobot. 2016. "Cobot - managing coworking spaces", accessed January, 2018. https://www.cobot.me/

7. Cobot. 2016. "Cobot Support Center". https://www.cobot.me/support#guides

8. Cohere Bandwidth. 2016. "Band Rehearsal Space", accessed January, 2016. https://coherebandwidth.com/

9. Cohere, LLC. 2016. "Cohere". http://coherecommunity.com/

10. CoPass. 2016. "CoPass", accessed January, 2018. https://copass.org/network

11. Cottle, Frank. 2016. "A Foundation for Change: A single global voicex." Global Coworking Unconference Conference, Los Angeles, May 6. http://canada.gcuc.co/wp-content/uploads/2016/presentations/Foundation%20and%20Giving%20-%20Frank%20Cottle.pdf

12. Hamilton, Anita. 2014. The Public Library Wants To Be Your Office. Accessed January, 2018. http://www.fastcompany.com/3034143/the-public-library-wants-to-be-your-office

13. HeraHub. 2017. "Hera Hub: Workspace for Women", accessed January 2015. http://herahub.com/

14. Hillman, Alex. 2013. "Indy Hall 2012: Reviewing Our Coworking Community by the Numbers." *Alex Hillman*, Feb 4. http://dangerouslyawesome.com/2013/02/indy-hall-2012-reviewing-our-coworking-community-by-the-numbers/

15. Hillman, Alex. 2016. The problem with the coworking industry in 2016. *New Worker Magazine*. Accessed January, 2018. http://newworker.co/mag/the-problem-with-the-coworking-industry-in-2016/

16. Hoffice. 2017. "Hoffice: Come and work at someone's home", accessed January, 2018. http://hoffice.nu/en/

17. Horowitz, Sara. 2012. *The Freelancer's Bible*. New York: Workman Publishing.

18. Jelly. 2017. "Jelly: Working together is more fun for everyonw!", accessed January, 2018. http://workatjelly.com/

19. Johnson, Cat. 2015. 7 Essential Coworking Resources for Digital Nomads. *Shareable*. Accessed January, 2018. http://www.shareable.net/blog/7-essential-coworking-resources-for-digital-nomads

20. Johnson, Cat. 2016. Look Out, Coworking. Here Comes Big Money. *Shareable*. Accessed January, 2018. http://www.shareable.net/blog/look-out-coworking-here-comes-big-money

21. Kane, Lori, Tabitha Borchardt, and Bas de Baar. 2015. *Reimagination Stations: Creating a Game-Changing In-Home Coworking Space*: Lori Kane.

22. Kwiatkowski, Angel, and Beth Buczynski. 2011. "Coworking: Building Community as a Space Catalyst." Ft. Collins: Cohere Coworking. http://coherecommunity.com/shop/coworking-building-community-as-a-space-catalyst (accessed January, 2018).

23. LiquidSpace. 2017. "The LiquidSpace Network", accessed January, 2018. https://liquidspace.com/network-for-office-space

24. Make Shift Boston. 2016. "Make Shift Boston", accessed January, 2018. http://makeshiftboston.org/space

25. Meetup. 2017. "Find Your People - Meetup", accessed January, 2018. https://www.meetup.com/

26. Miller, Anna Bergren. 2014. Enspiral: Changing the Way Social Entrepreneurs Do Business. *Sharable*. Accessed January, 2018. http://www.shareable.net/blog/enspiral-changing-the-way-social-entrepreneurs-do-business

27. NextSpace. 2016. "NextSpace", accessed January, 2016. http://nextspace.us/

28. Nexudus. 2017. "Nexudus: The white-label coworking software", accessed January, 2018. http://coworking.nexudus.com/en

29. Office Nomads. 2017. "The Nadine Project", accessed January, 2018. http://nadineproject.org/

30. Olma, Sebastian. 2012. "The Serendipity Machine: A Disruptive Business Model for Society 3.0." https://www.seats2meet.com/downloads/The_Serendipity_Machine.pdf (accessed January 2018).

31. Our Enspiral Spaces. 2015. "Enspiral Space", accessed January, 2015. https://enspiral.com/our-spaces/

32. Phoenix Public Library. 2016. "About hive", accessed January, 2018. https://www.phoenixpubliclibrary.org/hive/Pages/About-hive.aspx

33. Proximity Space. 2017. "Connecting Communities & Coworking Spaces", accessed January, 2018. https://proximity.space/

34. Seats2Meet. 2016. "Our Locations", accessed January, 2018. https://www.seats2meet.com/en/locations

35. Seats2Meet. 2016. "Seats2Meet - Connecting and empowering you to excel", accessed January, 2018. https://www.seats2meet.com/en

36. Seattle Collaborative Space Alliance. 2016. "Seattle Collaborative Space Alliance (SCSA)", accessed January, 2018. http://collaborativespaces.org/

37. SLO Makerspace. 2016. "Cubicles - SLO Makerspace", accessed January, 2018. http://www.slomakerspace.com/cubicles/

38. Surman, Tonya. 2013. "Building Social Entrepreneurship through the Power of Coworking." *Innovations: Technology, Governance, Globalization* 8 (3-4):189-195. doi: 10.1162/INOV_a_00195. http://dx.doi.org/10.1162/INOV_a_00195

39. The Centre for Social Innovation. 2016. "Culture | The Centre for Social Innovation", accessed January, 2018. https://socialinnovation.org/culture/

40. The Coworking Wiki. 2015. "Coworking Manifesto (global - for the world) " *The Coworking Wiki.* http://wiki.coworking.org/w/page/35382594/Coworking%20Manifesto%20%28global%20-%20for%20the%20world%29

41. The League of Extraordinary Coworking Spaces. 2016. "The League of Extraordinary Coworking Spaces", accessed January, 2018. http://lexc.org/

42. The Left Bank Project. 2016. "Hive at the Left Bank", accessed January, 2018. http://leftbankproject.com/hive/

43. University of Illinois. 2017. "Enterpriseworks Affiliates Program - Research Park", accessed January, 2018. http://www.researchpark.illinois.edu/resources/enterpriseworks-affiliate-program

44. WeWork. 2015. "WeWork: Create Your Life's Work", accessed January, 2018. https://www.wework.com/

45. Work and Play. 2016. "Work and Play", accessed January, 2018. http://www.workandplaynj.com/

Chapter 5: Community Management: Coworking Leadership Practices

Workspace and infrastructure are necessary but not sufficient for a successful coworking space; coworking is all about *community*. A coworking space must bring together a group of independent workers who talk, collaborate, create, and thrive together. This community does not happen spontaneously: "[s]omeone *must* step forward" ([12], p. 12).

It might be said that operating a coworking space is about "operating a community". One of the most interesting developments out of the contemporary coworking movement has been the emergence of a cadre of community leaders, who are equipped with a growing body of practical methodology to create and sustain communities of independent workers.

This chapter examines this leadership role. The first section examines the professional role of community manager, which has many alternative job titles. While there is no one single correct approach, there is a surprisingly broad consensus on how coworking communities should work and about the general role of coworking community leaders.

The coworking community should have a friendly, vibrant culture, and it should be a mutually supportive group characterized by many spontaneous conversations and collaborations. To help the workers achieve this, the leader should actively engage with workers as peers by making introductions, practicing hospitality, teaching the group's story, and generally modeling the values of the community culture.

The second section looks at the growing body of how-to and training materials created by and for coworking community leaders. These texts display a confident and pragmatic approach, which is all the more remarkable because it has developed bottom up.

While there are no formal schools or degrees to learn this profession, coworking leadership practices draw on and are influenced by a variety of sources. The third section sketches how coworking leaders have borrowed, consciously or not.

Some of the most important influences are the practices of digital social media communities. Many coworkers are digital natives, and a coworking space is often a physical instantiation of a virtual social network. Coworking community leaders also borrow from corporate Human Resources, community organizing, and even psychotherapy. In addition, coworking has an element of improv theater, in which the community leader invites workers to participate in an ongoing story about the new way of working.

5.1. Coworking Leadership: A New Job with Many Possible Job Titles

The contemporary coworking movement has seen the emergence of a cadre of leaders who not only manage the office facilities but also manage the community of workers who inhabit a space. These professionals typically work for or own the coworking space. However, these managers are also immersed in the community of workers.

This position is an interesting new kind of job, combining features of a number of existing occupations. The job has responsibilities of a conventional office manager, elements of a corporate Human Resources officer, and a variety of difficult to classify tasks such as matchmaking collaborations between workers, problem solving, informal conversation, and organizing social events.

This position has similar a variety of job titles, like *community manager* or *community wrangler,* both of which are titles found originally in digital communities. Alternative job titles might be more whimsical to reflect a lighthearted, friendly approach. Tony Bacigalupo called himself "mayor of New Work City" [4], Tonya Surman describes herself as a "community animator" at the Centre for Social Innovation (CSI) [23], and Angel Kwiatkowski and Beth Buczynsk describe their role as a "space catalyst" for Cohere coworking [12]. Others describe their own roles in nurturing terms such as the "mother of the space," "conductor," or "social gardener" [16]. Alex Hillman, rejecting the term *community manager*, suggests that the role is similar to a *tummler*, evoking a figure from twentieth-century resorts [7]. Table 5.1 lists commonly used job titles.

Some coworking spaces are described as "curated" by the operators, which means that they act deliberately to form a collection of workers following an implicit or explicit understanding of the nature of the desired community. Like the curator of a museum, gallery, or zoo, a coworking curator selects workers to fill out his or her collection.

Table 5.1 Example Job Titles for Coworking Community Leaders

Job Title	Reference
Community manager	[17, 29] and many others
Community wrangler	many
Community connector	[28, 22] and others
Curator	[13, 15, 1] and others
Mayor (of New Work City)	[4]
Space captain	[4]
Minister of fun	[4]
Community animator	[23]
Space catalyst	[12]
Madame	[12]
mother of the space	[16]
conductor	[16]
social gardener	[16]
Community facilitator	[7]
Community cultivator	[7]
Community activator	[7]
Tummler	[7]
Host	[16]

An example of one such position is a *community manager* for the coworking chain *NextSpace* [17]. A want ad from March 2016 includes the following job description:

> We focus on two things. The first is cultivating community. The second is running world class workspaces. Your job is to do whatever it takes to make sure these two things are functioning at the highest possible level. In service of these goals we find ourselves doing all kinds of tasks. Here's a short list in no particular order: showing potential members the space and explaining who we are and how we operate, facilities management, signing up new members, making connections, planning and hosting events, helping members take their businesses to the next level, updating our membership database, ordering supplies, making coffee, marketing (including that social media stuff), owning the financial health of your space, and taking on big picture projects as needed by the company as a whole. Basically, you can consider anything that involves creating a stronger community or a better workspace on your list of responsibilities, regardless of what the task is. Oh, and you get to travel a bit too. We have eight different locations and we don't want you to be a stranger! ([18, 19], accessed March 2016)

The NextSpace job has elements of a conventional office manager (facilities management, ordering supplies, "owning the financial health" of the site), combined with elements of a conventional human resources officer (onboarding new workers, keeping a database of workers), as well as public relations and with unspecified additional functions to "strengthen the community." The list of community-centered responsibilities really sets the job apart, including making connections, planning and hosting events, and helping members.

Janet Merkel studied the role of *hosts* in coworking spaces, who curate the space and its community [19]. She gives one of the clearest descriptions of the role of coworking space leader:

> The host's activities of curatorial practice can be summarized as assembling and arranging (people, spaces, objects), creating and signifying new meanings (collaboration, community, sustainability, openness, and accessibility), reframing (work differently), caring (enabling community) and exhibiting (the work space and its community), all in order to create new work-related and social experiences in the city. ([16], p. 131)

These hosts are also important because they "embed their activity in narratives and stories" ([16], p. 132)—that is, they help define coworking for both workers and the general public. Merkel describes this role as hospitality, a term usually applied to hotels, restaurants, and resorts:

> Hosts use different social and physical strategies to animate and stimulate interaction and collaboration among coworkers. Socially, they initiate events and regular meetings, or develop formats for introducing coworkers to one another such as blogs where new members are presented and can meet, or bulletin boards at the entrance where members can put up a profile or search for help and specific skills. Or hosts get members in the coworking spirit just by talking, connecting, recommending, and caring in their daily work. They report that eating together, such as having lunch together or clearing the fridge on Fridays, has proven to be the most effective socialization mechanism. Additionally, there are organized talks by members, as well as seminars and courses. Educational programs are a common feature of almost every space. These courses and peer-to-peer learning groups cater to the coworkers' interests and needs, but are usually also accessible for the larger public, without requiring a membership card. ([16], pp. 129–30)

The host both facilitates collaboration and "translates coworking values into the space" ([16], p. 125). Merkel's description indicates both the goals of this position and the instrumental approach to achieving them. The goals emphasize efforts to create and support the social community among the workers—for example, "to animate and stimulate interaction and collaboration among coworkers" and "introducing coworkers to one another."

These goals are combined with a pragmatic approach, explicitly employing "social and physical strategies." The host "initiates" group events and individual meetings and directly interacts with the workers, "talking, connecting, recommending, and caring."

Merkel's description of the functions and role of a coworking host is corroborated by explanations offered by coworking leaders themselves.

Indy Hall cofounder Alex Hillman echoes many of the same points emphasized by Merkel. Hillman himself eschews the term *community manager*, complaining that "just hearing the word 'manager' suggests a hierarchy and a control which is unnatural in communities" [16]. He also rejects the "cruise director mindset" implied by Merkel term *host*, which "does too much" and is too centralized. A group culture that depends on the presence of the manager and a few individuals is fragile and undesirable. His goal is to "create a system that helps a particular culture grow, even when you're not in the room."

Tony Bacigalupo, Mayor of the New Work City coworking space, leaves the curation to the community itself. He says that the goal of the leader is to "steer your culture in the right direction." Recounting his experience, he describes principles and "simple systems" that "made potentially difficult things easier" and "fostered a sense of trust and created space for healthier culture" ([7], p. 11).

Tonya Surman of The Centre for Social Innovation (CSI) describes her role as a *community animator*, which is "a cross between a triage nurse, a guidance counselor, and a potluck organizer" ([4], p. 192). The CSI practices what she calls "radical hospitality," which is intended to "make peoples' lives happier." This hospitality is "conscious and careful animation," which introduces members to each other to "reveal the assets in the ecosystem" and also includes training, mentorship, and other resources.

Angel Kwiatkowski and Beth Buczynsk, of Cohere Coworking describe their roles in building the community as a "space catalyst" [23]. A space catalyst is "a daily fixture in the community" who seeks to "help people get through barriers, overcome roadblocks, and examine the larger context of what they're doing in the world" ([12], p. 14).

5.2. Pragmatic Tools: Confident How-to Books and Training

These descriptions of coworking leadership show that there is a growing body of expert practitioners with a common view of the goals and a set of pragmatic techniques. These leaders are "conscious and careful" (Surman), employing tools, techniques, and processes to "catalyze" (Kwiatkowski and Buczynsk) and "steer" the culture (Bacigalupo).

There is no formal school for coworking community leadership yet, but there are a growing number of blogs, "how to" books, and other training materials. This emerging culture of cultural leaders is one of the more remarkable features of contemporary coworking.

Tony Bacigalupo on Steering the Culture and Cotivation

Tony Bacigalupo describes his approach to community management in his book *No More Sink Full of Mugs* [12]. The bulk of the book is eight principles and twelve simple systems that "made potentially difficult things easier." His basic principles describe a self-governing group of people who respect and trust each other.

To steer the group toward these principles, he describes "12 Simple Systems for Happy, Empowered Communities" ([4], Chapter 2). These recommendations for community leaders are phrased as things "we," the community, do:

1. We celebrate when people clear the sink.
2. We let members be in charge of the coffee.
3. We give everyone a way to connect with each other through an online discussion group.
4. We're intentional but not overly pushy about onboarding new members.
5. We hold a monthly Welcome Aboard Member Meeting (WAMM).
6. We let the members start and stop their own memberships.
7. We make our business hours malleable.
8. We rely on our culture and our values when we encounter people who we fear may not be a good fit.

9. We don't charge extra for printing—or anything else.
10. We let members book our large conference room online.
11. We let members book smaller meeting rooms in the space.
12. We offer members a way to help run the place. ([4], Chapter 2)

In recent years, Bacigalupo has formalized some of his leadership practices in the *Cotivation* program (in collaboration with Susan Dorsch of Office Nomads [4]). This program is designed to help coworkers succeed as independent, freelance workers.

> [I]t is our responsibility to give our members more than just an office to work in and other people to be around. We have the opportunity to connect them to support systems they need to not just survive but truly thrive. [4]

The program addresses the challenge that an independent worker lacks the social context of colleagues who provide feedback, encouragement, and motivation. Their company sells materials and training packages to enable coworking spaces to set up their own Cotivation self-help meetings [20]. Workers join a regular group for mutual support and a sense of belonging. A Cotivation group meets weekly "to set goals and revisit previous commitments, so every participant has a chance to make progress with the help of fellow coworkers."

Cotivation is said to offer the participants (from [5]):

- an invitation to participate;
- a safe space to get vulnerable;
- much-needed external accountability;
- a sense of belonging;
- valuable feedback from a diverse group of peers; and
- a serious sense of achievement.

These weekly meetings resemble and are a substitute for team meetings held in conventional organizations, though perhaps without the tension due to evaluation by supervisors or competition from peers. This program also draws on concepts from group dynamics, problem-solving processes, and even group therapy.

Gradin Franzén and Lindholm's Hoffice

Christofer Gradin Franzén and Johline Lindholm have created what they call Hoffice (home + office), which combines home coworking with a semi-structured process that resembles an encounter group or therapy session [11, 5]. Independent workers connect with each other to arrange a day of coworking convened in a private home.

As in the case of Cotivation, the group is designed to be both supportive and to hold each worker accountable for their own tasks. "The two roles that are essential for a Hoffice [are] the host and the facilitator" [5]. The host is tasked with providing the space and arranging catering.

The Hoffice facilitator runs the process throughout the workday. The opening meeting is a circle, including mindfulness exercises and sharing of goals for the day. These goals are tracked and reported throughout the day, holding the worker accountable within a friendly group. At the end of the day, accomplishments are celebrated at a communal meal.

The term facilitator is adopted from group therapy, and the work process resembles some forms of psychological therapy. This no doubt reflects Gradin Franzén's professional training to be a psychotherapist, as well as his interests in collective intelligence and a gift economy [30, 8].

Tonya Surman on Community Animation

Tonya Surman of The Centre for Social Innovation (CSI) (in Toronto and other cities) describes her approach to cultivating community in their space. In *Building Social Entrepreneurship through the Power of Coworking*, Suman explains that social spaces should "warm, welcoming, and buzzing with activity" in order to create interpersonal bonds and group identity ([23], p. 191). A community is cultivated through "conscious and careful animation" by one or more community animators.

Surman describes three things that make a community "come to life" ([23], p. 193-4).:

1. Curation—recruit people who share a set of values and interests
2. Culture—"innovation, creativity, permission, fun, and authenticity" as well as mutual support
3. Connection—the social network in the space

The CSI is a not-for-profit accelerator dedicated to "catalyzing social innovation" and generating social enterprises. They seek to "open source" their model, including coworking, so that others may emulate their success.

To this end, they have issued a series of reports [24, 26, 25] and other publications describing their approach.

Kwiatkowski and Buczynsk on Space Catalysts

Angel Kwiatkowski and Beth Buczynsk of Cohere Coworking have published a variety of training materials describing coworking community leadership. In *Coworking: Building Community as a Space Catalyst* [23], they explain that, analogous to chemical catalysts, a space catalyst speeds and increases production of community products. This sort of catalyst is essential for a successful coworking community because

> [c]oworking provides a way to be independent and connect with others, but just finding a room with desks and internet won't cut it. Someone *must* step forward to create and hold the space where productive work and a saturated sense of community can happen at any time. ([24, 26, 25], p. 12)

They provide a variety of how-to tips, including many suggestions about techniques, tools, and best practices for facilities management, marketing, and so on. But, as implied by the title, the critical functions must be facilitating the social interactions of the workers. "Catalysts that envision themselves being a daily fixture in the community will have the ability and patience to help people get through barriers, overcome roadblocks, and examine the larger context of what they're doing in the world" ([12], p. 14).

Rachael Gursky on Hospitality

Rachael Gursky holds the title "Head of Hospitality" for the Industrious coworking chain [12] and views coworking as very similar to hotels and other hospitality businesses:

> Just like hotels create an experience for their guests each night through service and product offerings, we create an experience for our members each day. We don't just provide our members with a place and tools to run their business; we create an atmosphere that makes our members feel excited to come to work. (Gursky, quoted in [12])

The experience is created through a combination of features, including "sophisticated music, high quality café offerings, and friendly community managers." She says that the community managers are the most important element. "They're the ones that best know the members, the ones that make sure that everything is up to par for them, the ones that organize and host events" (Gursky quoted in [10]). This role is so crucial that Industrious prefers to hire workers with experience in hospitality (such as hotels) and then train them to operate an office.

Alex Hillman on Community Management

Indy Hall [3] cofounder Alex Hillman has written and spoken extensively on coworking and community leadership. He says his goal as a coworking leader is to "create a system that helps a particular culture grow, even when you're not in the room" [3]. Like Merkel, he stresses the informality and social nature of the job and the deliberate, instrumental approach toward these goals. The leader both tells the story and works hard to induce workers to *enact* the story.

Hillman offers an array of materials and consulting, including biweekly group coaching sessions called "The Indy Hall Braintrust" [9]. He describes some of the topics of interest to this "community of professional community builders":

- Improving the impact of the hard work you put into events
- Boosting member participation and engagement
- How to give a coworking tour that helps people understand coworking
- Resolving conflicts—and spotting them early!
- Tips and tricks for helping teams of people integrate with your community [7]

Hillman dislikes some of the common titles for this role, especially *community manager* and *host*. He suggests something like a *tummler*, a term from the practices at twentieth-century resorts in the Catskills [27]. The role of a *tummler* is

> to encourage people participating in the dance floor—Tummlers take a very particular approach to "warm" the crowd.

> They cruise the party. They listen, and they observe. They ask questions, and they earn trust.

They meet people at the edges of the crowd, connect with them, and then slowly help those people discover their own way into the mix. [7]

This is the essence of what the leader of a coworking space should do, according to Hillman. He has given us a very vivid image of a coworking leader trying to get coworkers to "get up and dance" with each other.

5.3. Perspectives on Coworking Leadership: Influences and Sources

Coworking communities are diverse and decentralized; each community is different. There is no school or textbook to teach coworking management, and community leaders often come from the community itself. Nevertheless, as discussed in this chapter, a cadre of professional community leaders has emerged, and these leaders share similar philosophy and techniques.

Coworking leaders employ an eclectic mix of techniques, many borrowed from other contexts. In many cases, these connections are not explicitly acknowledged, and individual leaders may not even be aware of the conceptual history of their practice. Nevertheless, it is possible to point to some of these connections.

First, community leaders tell the story of coworking and what it means to cowork: coworking represents *the future of work*, enabled by digital technology and designed to fit the contemporary gig economy, and untethered from geographical and organizational bounds. Displaced by the 2008 crash, millennials "had no place to go," and many would not want to go back to a corporate office, were that an option [6]. The missing piece is the social community of workers and the corporate culture of a conventional workplace. Community leaders seek to create and sustain this community and its culture.

The core of coworking communities and their leaders are mostly digital natives immersed in Internet culture. This background leads many to feel comfortable with conventions and practices familiar from digital communities. For example, coworking communities value the open collaboration and sharing found in open-source software projects, peer-to-peer social networks, and digital collaborations such as crowdsourcing and crowdfunding.

Indeed, for many workers, coworking is essentially an online community augmented with a physical place to have face-to-face interactions. Given this connection and the cultural milieu of the workers, it is not surprising that conception about the role of community manager has migrated from online communities to physical coworking communities.

In addition, many pragmatic techniques adopted by coworking community leaders are drawn from other sources, including corporate human resources, academic organizational psychology, community organizing, and even new-age self-help. In each case, leaders apply these practices to build communities and teams and to assure the satisfaction and success of individual workers.

Community leaders for coworking communities have many functions that are very similar to Human Resources professionals in conventional organizations. The leader is responsible for recruiting and onboarding new workers, as well as ongoing relations between the worker and the operator of the space. The leader also strives to maintain a healthy and happy working environment with positive relations among workers. The leader also helps individual workers to be productive through mentoring, training, and introductions.

The Cotivation process clearly illustrates how coworking communities can synthesize the benefits of belonging to an organization for workers with no formal affiliation with each other or the workspace. The Cotivation process includes elements found in many organizational team processes, including goal setting, peer feedback, and weekly progress meetings [7]. Essentially, a Cotivation group is a project team that doesn't have a project but meets for the purpose of having a team.

To foster a successful and healthy community of workers, many coworking community leaders draw on democratic spirit and decision-making processes practices favored by community activists and political organizers. Like digital communities—and in sharp contrast to corporate hierarchy— many coworking leaders encourage bottom-up, autonomous decision making and consensus seeking.

For example, Tony Bacigalupo instructs leaders to "[e]mpower people to handle things themselves wherever possible" [14]. Alex Hillman says, "It's your job to help community members understand that everyone shares that responsibility for culture" [11, 5].

Most coworking leaders are also concerned with improving the welfare of the individual workers, starting with efforts to mitigate some of the social isolation of independent workers and fostering a sense of belonging to the community. They may employ concepts and techniques borrowed from social science, group dynamics, and psychotherapy. Many coworking leaders have also been influenced by the immense amount of popular literature on self-help, business motivation, and pop psychology.

For example, a coworking leader may be a mentor or business coach for workers, teaching work practices and personal skills and providing support and feedback. This coaching may include motivational slogans and pep talks, but it also can include peer support groups, such as Cotivation [4] or Hoffice [7].

Many people consider coworking to be a segment of the hospitality industry, and so it is not surprising that some coworking leaders draw from hotel and convention management. A hospitality company, such as a hotel or restaurant, should create an experience. As Rachael Gursky of Industrious says, "friendly community managers" are the most critical part of such an experience because they welcome and are friendly toward all guests and "create an atmosphere that makes our members feel excited to come to work" [2].

In this vein, Hillman takes the analogy beyond hospitality and into show business. The goal, he argues, is to have the guests run the show themselves. The leader should not only lead the workers to feel excited to come to work, but get them to get up and dance, to *enact the role* of coworker.

The leader is one who "spin[s] stories and new meanings from their own activity, the coworkers and the specific space" ([21], p.132). Spreitzer and others describe "three pathways whereby members experienced a sense of community: espousing, learning, enacting" [3]. The leader is a teacher who models how to cowork, tells the heroic story of the new way of work, and invites each worker to enact his or her own part in the story.

As in improv theater, the leader both acts in and directs the action. He or she manages the set and creates situations to evoke and advance the story. For example, community social events are not just business opportunities; they are occasions to display the values and behaviors of the coworking community and to tell stories.

5.4. Conclusion

The leadership practices of community managers are critical to the success of coworking and coworkers, both by creating and sustaining the community and by telling and enacting the culture of the community.

This chapter has described the emerging philosophy and practices of coworking community leaders. While different leaders have their own idiosyncratic approaches, there is surprising agreement about and consistency in leadership practices across many different coworking communities.

A class of professional leaders has emerged to "manage" coworking communities. These leaders embrace a variety of job titles, like curator, community manager, or one of many other options. Whatever the title, these leaders employ an array of techniques drawn from digital social media, conventional office management, Human Resources, and the hospitality industry: greeting new members, matchmaking, fostering friendly conversation, problem solving, and organizing social events.

In Alex Hillman's memorable image, he or she acts as a *tummler*, someone who works the crowd to get everyone out on the dance floor.

Chapter References

1. 1628. 2017. "1628 | A curated co-working space", accessed January, 2018. http://www.1628ltd.com/
2. Amador, Ceci. 2016. "How Coworking Changes your City." *GCUC Blog+Press*, March 29. http://usa.gcuc.co/how-coworking-changes-your-city/
3. Amador, Cecilia. 2016. "Learn About Hospitality from the Operator that Got it Right." *AllWork*, April 6. https://allwork.space/2016/04/learn-about-hospitality-from-the-operator-that-got-it-right/
4. Bacigalupo, Tony. 2015. "No More Sink Full of Mugs." New York: No More Sink Full of Mugs. https://sellfy.com/p/IBtB/ (accessed January, 2018).
5. Cotivation. 2017
. "Cotivation - Collaborative motivation groups for coworking spaces", accessed January, 2018. http://cotivation.co/
6. Dictionary.com. 2016. "tummler", accessed January, 2018. http://www.dictionary.com/browse/tummler
7. Hillman, Alex. 2014. "To build a strong community, stop "community managing", be a Tummler instead." *Alex Hillman*, April 20. http://dangerouslyawesome.com/2014/04/community-management-tummling-a-tale-of-two-mindsets/
8. Hoffice. 2017. "Hoffice: Come and work at someone's home", accessed January, 2018. http://hoffice.nu/en/
9. Independents Hall LLC. 2016. "Coworking in Philadelphia - Indy Hall - a Community and Workspace - Est. 2006", accessed January, 2018. http://www.indyhall.org/
10. Industrious. 2017. "Coworking Redefined", accessed January, 2018. https://www.industriousoffice.com/
11. Johnson, Cat. 2015. Cotivation Helps Freelancers Succeed Through Mutual Accountability. *Shareable*. Accessed January, 2018. http://www.shareable.net/blog/cotivation-helps-freelancers-succeed-through-mutual-accountability
12. Kwiatkowski, Angel, and Beth Buczynski. 2011. "Coworking: Building Community as a Space Catalyst." Ft. Collins: Cohere Coworking. http://coherecommunity.com/shop/coworking-building-community-as-a-space-catalyst (accessed January, 2018).
13. Link Coworking. 2017. "Link Coworking — Bringing People Together", accessed January, 2018. http://www.linkcoworking.com/
14. Liquid Talent. 2015. "Dude, Where's My Drone: The future of work and what you can do to prepare for it."

https://www.dropbox.com/s/405kr9keucv97gw/LiquidTalentFoWE book.pdf?dl=0 (accessed January, 2018).

15. Matrix Coworking. 2017. "Matrix Coworking", accessed January, 2018. http://www.matrixcbsolutions.com/en

16. Merkel, Janet. 2015. "Coworking in the city." *Ephemera* 15 (1):121

17. NextSpace. 2016. "NextSpace", accessed January, 2016. http://nextspace.us/

18. NextSpace. 2016. "We're Hiring Community Builders", accessed March, 2016. http://nextspace.us/2016/02/22/were-hiring-sf/

19. NextSpace. 2017. "Careers At NextSpace", accessed March, 2016. http://nextspace.us/careers

20. Office Nomads. 2016. "Office Nomads", accessed January, 2018. http://officenomads.com/

21. Renascent Hospitality LLC. 2016. "Serendipity Labs Coworking Coming to Columbus", accessed January, 2018. http://www.renascenthospitality.com/Blog/174748/Serendipity-Labs-Coworking-Coming-to-Columbus

22. Sub Urban Co-Working. 2017. "Sub Urban Co-Working", accessed January, 2018. http://www.suburban.org.nz/

23. Surman, Tonya. 2013. "Building Social Entrepreneurship through the Power of Coworking." *Innovations: Technology, Governance, Globalization* 8 (3-4):189-195. doi: 10.1162/INOV_a_00195. http://dx.doi.org/10.1162/INOV_a_00195

24. The Centre for Social Innovation. 2016. Emergence: The Story of The Centre for Social Innovation. http://socialinnovation.ca/sites/socialinnovation.ca/files/Emergence_The_Story_of_the_Centre_for_Social_Innovation.pdf.

25. The Centre for Social Innovation. 2016. Proof: How Shared Spaces are Changing the World. http://socialinnovation.ca/sites/socialinnovation.ca/files/Proof_How_shared_spaces_are_changing_the_world_.pdf.

26. The Centre for Social Innovation. 2016. Rigour: How-To Create World-Changing Spaces. http://socialinnovation.ca/sites/socialinnovation.ca/files/Rigour_How_to_create_World-Changing_Shared_Spaces_.pdf.

27. The Indy Hall Braintrust. 2017. "The club for professional community builders ", accessed January, 2018. https://theindyhallway.com/braintrust/

28. Think Big Coworking. 2017. "Think Big Coworking", accessed January, 2018. http://thinkbigcoworking.com/

29. WeWork. 2015. "WeWork: Create Your Life's Work", accessed January, 2018. https://www.wework.com/

30. Wolf, Andeas. 2016. How to "Hoffice" with Other Freelancers for More Health, Happiness and Productivity. *Sharable*. Accessed January, 2018. http://www.shareable.net/blog/how-to-hoffice-with-other-freelancers-for-more-health-happiness-and-productivity

Part III. How Well Does It Work? And Why?

Chapter 6: What Are the Benefits of Coworking?

6.1. Introduction

Previous chapters described the needs that coworking addresses (low-cost infrastructure, respite from loneliness) and the many ways that coworking has been organized. For most workers, the most important feature is participation in a community of peers. The community is sustained in part by pragmatic community leaders.

This chapter turns to the question, how well does coworking work?

Specifically, "What are the benefits of coworking?"

This question can be broken down into two pieces.

> **What does coworking do for workers?** How do workers themselves benefit from coworking?

> **What does coworking do for work practices and outcomes**? How does coworking improve the work done?

This chapter looks at three types of sources that address these questions: organized studies, testimony from workers, and materials that explain how to operate a coworking space and community. Each of these sources is imperfect and incomplete, but taken together they tell a consistent story. (The Chapter Appendix lists the sources used in this chapter.)

Overall, it seems that workers are generally satisfied with their coworking space and community and report a variety of benefits from coworking. Table 6.1 summarizes the main benefits that are supported by all the sources. The benefits to coworkers themselves include satisfaction, social support, and a feeling of belonging to a community. Workers also may produce better work, including improved productivity, collaboration with other workers, and more business opportunities. The following sections review some of the evidence for these benefits.

Table 6.1. Summary of Benefits of Coworking

Benefits to Workers	
	Satisfaction (happiness)
	Social support (Relief from isolation and loneliness, friendship)
	Feeling of belonging to a community
Benefits to their work and performance	
	Improved productivity, better work, new skills
	Collaboration and creativity
	Business opportunities

6.2. Evidence from Surveys and Studies

One source of information about coworking spaces and coworkers is a growing number of surveys, both commercial and academic. Overall, a dozen studies point to an array of benefits from coworking. Each of these studies uses some combination of interviews and questionnaires to gather information from samples of coworkers, community leaders, and operators.

These studies offer some of the best information about coworkers and the experience of coworking, as well as statistical trends in coworking spaces over time and in different places.

Findings: Benefits to Workers

First and foremost, every survey has found that, in general, workers are very satisfied by coworking and that coworking makes coworkers happy. For example, the 2015 *Deskmag* survey of 1,000 or more coworkers around the world reports that 89 percent of coworkers "reported they are happier" [53]. The Centre for Social Innovation (CSI) survey of 80 members reports that 76 percent agree that membership at CSI has made them a happier person [54]. Spreitzer and her colleagues' online survey of several hundred coworkers found that coworkers reported extremely high levels of "thriving" [52].

Second, workers find social support in their coworking space. In this age of continuous digital connection, workers still enjoy and desire the physical presence of other workers. A coworking space offers such face-to-face connections, which Klaas describes as a "respite from our isolation" for these independent workers [34]. *Deskmag* reports that 83 percent of coworkers say "they are less lonely" [53]. The 2016 *Deskmag* lists "interaction with others" as the number-one reason to select a specific coworking space [16]. Other studies confirm the importance of conviviality [27, 51].

Many coworkers gain more than just companionship; they feel a sense of community. Spreitzer says that coworkers like coworking because "[t]hey feel part of a community" [52]. The 2016 *Deskmag* survey lists the second and third reasons to choose a coworking space (after "interaction with others") to be "a community" and "like-minded people" [16].

The 2017 *Deskmag* survey has the same items in slightly different order: "A community" is number 1, "like-minded people" is number 3, and "interaction with others" is fifth. [9]. Number 4 is a new item: "a social and enjoyable atmosphere." All of these features rank above infrastructure and fees.

This sense of community comes not only from interaction with "like-minded" peers, but from active participation *"espousing, learning, enacting"* membership in the local community (per Garnett et al. [20]). Spreitzer suggests that this participation gives their work additional meaning [52]. Similarly, Surman reports that the workers at the CSI feel a sense of belonging, which gives additional meaning to their work ([57], p. 65).

Findings: Benefits to Work Performance

Studies of coworking also report an array of benefits to the work performance and productivity of coworkers. For example, one *Deskmag* survey reported that 69 percent said they "feel more successful since joining a coworking space," and a similar number said coworking "improved their professional success" [53]. Surman reports something similar: that 87 percent of members feel that working at CSI has "improved the quality of their professional life" [54]. These subjective assessments suggest a common set of specific benefits underlying the perceived improvements.

First of all, the community of friendly peers help each other in a number of ways, both directly and indirectly. Simply being around other workers has positive psychological benefits. For example, the 2015 *Deskmag* survey reported that 84 percent were "more engaged and motivated when coworking" [53]. Spinuzzi reports that, among other interactions, workers received feedback and encouragement [51].

Coworkers also learn new technical and business skills from peers and from classes and presentations organized by the coworking community [51, 21]. The *Deskmag* survey reports 69 percent "learned new skills," and 68 percent "improved their existing skill set" [53]. Surman reports 67 percent of members said that membership has "enabled them to learn about new ideas, trends, information, techniques and/or audiences" [54]. Van de Vrande and Tempelaar report that coworking "contributes to improving current products and services" and "development of business skills" [63].

Many coworkers are freelancers and independent contractors who work from gig to gig. A coworking community is a business network for these freelancers, both for discovering new opportunities and for finding collaborators with needed skills [51, 21]. In the 2015 *Deskmag* survey, 64 percent of the respondents said "their coworking networking was a very important (26%) or important source of work (38%)" [53]. Van de Vrande and Tempelaar report that coworking contributes to "expanding customer networks" and finding gigs [63]. Hurry's 2012 thesis reports that almost all the coworkers "spoke of the Hub having a networking aspect*"* [27]. Surman reports that 85 percent of CSI members "have collaborated with at least one other member" [54].

The frequent personal interactions within an open and non-hierarchical, peer-to-peer community can lead to unexpected connections and collaborations. Hurry calls this "creative collisions" [27]. Van de Vrande and Tempelaar term it *collaborative innovation* [63]. Many coworkers refer to this as *serendipity*. In fact, Olma describes Seats2Meet coworking spaces as "The Serendipity Machine" [47].

Findings about Dissatisfied Coworkers

Most of the studies have sampled workers, operators, and community leaders who are currently coworking and satisfied with their current workspace. Workers who might be dissatisfied or might not have benefited from coworking are poorly represented in most of the studies and there is relatively little information about workers who choose not to cowork or who have tried coworking but no longer do so.

An exception to this is the 2012 *Deskmag* survey, which surveyed both "not-yet coworkers" and "ex-coworkers" [12]. In the first group, many workers might prefer to and might benefit from coworking but could not do so for various reasons. Some workers said they were unable to afford the fees or could not find coworking in their location. Others said their current employer prohibited using a coworking space.

Of the ex-cowokers, more than half had left for reasons other than dissatisfaction, including inability to pay fees, relocation, a new job, or business expansion. For these workers, coworking was a satisfactory, if temporary, stage in their work career.

Finally, some workers expressed dissatisfaction with coworking, at least the specific coworking space and community they had belonged to. Most cited dissatisfaction with the work environment, including lack of privacy (13%) and noisy environment (9%). Some were dissatisfied with the community, either "too little" community or a feeling of being forced into a community (i.e., "too much" community).

Caveats about Study Data

Drawing inferences from any survey or interview depends on details on the survey's methodology, especially how the sample is selected. Unfortunately, none of the studies discussed here have used scientific samples. To be fair, this shortcoming reflects the fundamental lack of knowledge about coworking and coworkers, because it is difficult to try to represent an unknown population.

With few exceptions, the surveys considered in this section have used some form of convenience samples. Some investigators have visited one or more nearby locations and interviewed workers found there. Others have used web surveys, unsystematically recruiting respondents via social media or word of mouth. Some of the studies collected data in close collaboration with the operator of the space.

A convenience sample is vulnerable to a variety of systematic errors and biases. To the degree that the respondents are self-selected, they may be quite unrepresentative of workers in general. In particular, it is important to bear in mind that the samples are very likely to be stacked with workers who are satisfied with coworking simply because the sample was drawn from current coworkers.

It also important to note that the samples used in the studies are small and, for the most part, not repeated over time. The data suggest that coworking communities grow rapidly, and membership changes continuously as individual workers join and leave the community. To the degree that this is true, it is difficult to draw conclusions about current or future trends from rapidly outdated snapshots of a community.

With these caveats in mind, there is still good reason to pay attention to these surveys. First of all, however limited, they are some of the best data that can be found. Altogether, there is interesting information from thousands of workers and hundreds of spaces in these studies. This may not be representative of all workers, but it is representative of some workers.

Second, the findings of the surveys have strong face validity: they are consistent with each other and with both anecdotes (i.e., self-reports) by workers and with instructional material designed to explain how to cowork. Therefore, it is reasonable to assume that the results from these surveys probably are representative of coworking communities and coworking spaces.

The limits and interpretation of these studies are discussed in more detail in chapter 7.

6.3. Anecdotal Evidence: Testimony from Coworkers

In addition to surveys and interviews, it is easy to find dozens and even hundreds of testimonials from coworkers themselves describing their experience and evaluation of coworking. The majority of personal reports from coworkers echo the main points reported by the studies described above. Coworking makes workers happy, and workers say they feel more productive, make important business connections, and feel part of a community.

There are also critiques of coworking. Some workers express dissatisfaction with one or more coworking experiences. They describe how a specific coworking space or community did not meet their needs and preferences. In addition, there are critiques of the perceived narrow demographics of some coworking spaces. These critiques echo similar concerns about the lack of diversity in the technology industry and the "digital divide" between haves and have-nots.

Reports from Satisfied Coworkers

There are many reports from satisfied coworkers. For example, Kwiatkowski and Buczynski [36] include brief statements from 30 happy coworkers. Jones, Sundsted, and Bacigalupo another dozen [31], Steve King another dozen [33], the Philadelphia studies [64, 39], and many coworking spaces offer statements from their members. The reports are generally similar, indicating that coworkers are happy, feel a part of a community, and benefit from belonging to a coworking space.

For one example, Melissa Mesku has published several articles describing her experiences coworking. She describes how she discovered her career as a freelancer and the intangible satisfactions of the "serendipity" she finds in her coworking space [44]:

> My first freelance client—I said I got this at my coworking space. But that's not the full story. The full story is *it had never even occurred to me to try doing freelance work* and then one day my friend at the coworking space was complaining about a client he didn't want disappoint [sic] but didn't want to take on, and *in conversation we both realized that I had the skills to take the client on instead.* He sent an email recommending me and within ten minutes I had my first client in what later became a full-blown career. [44]

Another piece describes choosing one coworking space over another. The two spaces had similar infrastructure, and indeed, she preferred one that might be an inferior physical space. The crucial difference was the community of workers. The first workplace was "seamless and dry": "I had become enamored with the place because of how swanky it looked and how smoothly it functioned, but I hadn't managed to get to know anyone." The second place was "ramshackle" and "ugly," but "I was welcome and immediately felt comfortable to be myself and to get to know everyone. Within a few days I felt the space to be my new home" [43].

Cat Johnson has thoughtful commentary, describing a similar migration from "a desk rental facility" to her "current home coworking space":

> I spent a year "coworking" in a desk rental facility. When I left, I barely knew anyone by name except the guy at the front desk. Compare that to my current home coworking space, where I am met with smiles and greetings from a diverse and supportive group of people whom I learn from daily and share, collaborate, cry, laugh, and work with. [30]

These selected comments suggest the tone and content of comments from dozens of satisfied coworkers around the world. Many workers say they are more productive, have learned valuable skills, and have made important connections in the coworking community. Nearly all are happy, primarily because they feel part of a friendly community, and many remark that they are less isolated and lonely.

Reports by Dissatisfied Coworkers

Not all workers have been satisfied with coworking, and some have expressed their dissatisfaction. Inevitably, a coworking community of supposedly like-minded peers will suit some workers and types of work better than others.

Some workers have tried several coworking spaces and prefer one workspace or community to another. As discussed in the previous section, Johnson, Mesku, and Kane describe dissatisfaction with particular coworking spaces but have found another space and community that they like. Their remarks include criticism that indicates a lack of social connection—for example, that the non-preferred space was "dry" where she "barely knew anyone by name."

One common source of dissatisfaction is that some workers *are* looking for inexpensive desk rental and have less interest in social support or amenities. For example, James Cropcho expresses discontent with some of his coworking experiences, finding the social interaction ("*water-cooler lollygagging and gossipy conversations*") distracting and detrimental for his productivity [6]: "*Having to politely navigate my way out of being an involuntary accomplice to others' procrastination is annoying, so I gave up and went back to working from coffeehouses.*"

He prefers temporary workspaces with very short-term occupancy, such as renting a desk for an hour, in one hour from now. This modus operandi has little commitment to community or serendipity.

Stefan Bhagwandin makes a similar criticism of what he calls "luxury" coworking spaces: "Flashy amenities and luxuries don't address the customer's core needs. People don't rent office space to relax or to feel like they're in a hotel; they do it to work" [3].

He argues that when the novelty of having "fun" in the coworking space wears off, workers will face a tradeoff between productivity and distractions. Clearly, Bhagwandin does not value conviviality or community as much as inexpensive, distraction-free workspace.

Some workers attribute dissatisfaction with particular coworking spaces to the demographic makeup of the community. As is the case in the technology industry overall, many coworking spaces are dominated by young, pale males. Such a community may not feel like peers or easily engender a sense of community for women, for some ethnic groups, for older workers, or others who do not fit comfortably into the culture. As Samara Lynn advises, in addition to the usual infrastructure, "Black startup owners may also want to search for co-working spaces with multiethnic staff and fellow entrepreneurs" ([38], p. 38).

Lori Kane reflects on the ethnic and socioeconomic dimensions of the coworking community, compared to the urban neighborhood. She described her dissatisfaction with otherwise outstanding coworking spaces she visited, which did not match the demographics of the city outside the door [32].

> I walked into the building, in through the doors, and up in to this lovely coworking space, and it was a sea of very young, white faces. I realized that in the Central District, my little neighborhood in Seattle, we could do better. [29]

This was "not at all what the walk through the diverse neighborhood primed me to expect" ([32], p. 9).

In recent years, more coworking spaces do indeed represent a variety of local urban neighborhoods, such as The Harlem Collective [61], Nebula (St Louis) [45], and Shift (Chicago) [60]. Of course, no workplace can suit every worker, no matter what the demographic makeup.

It is frequently noted that a coworking space that is "fun" for young male workers might be less attractive for older workers or women of any age. This hypothesis is partly supported by the development of female-oriented coworking spaces, such as Hera Hub [23], Women's Business Incubator [66], The Wing [61], One Roof [48], Thrive [62], and others. (On the other hand, Mesku suggests that a local coworking community might be a happy hunting ground for romance, especially for young working women [42].)

Caveats about Anecdotal Data

Together, these reports offer a picture of what workers like about coworking and what benefits they see from coworking. The picture needs to be considered carefully, of course, because many of the statements were obviously intended to be promotional materials.

It is important to note that these personal anecdotes are mostly based on experience at only one or at most a few specific coworking spaces, at one particular time and place. Some coworkers are very satisfied with the coworking space(s) they have encountered, others have been less satisfied, but these stories can't tell us about all coworking spaces or all workers.

Overall, these stories reveal what coworkers do and don't like about coworking. Satisfied coworkers report the same benefits described by the surveys and studies. Satisfied coworkers are happy, feel more productive, and benefit from belonging to a community of peers. At the same time, critiques of coworking indicate that one size does not fit all coworkers. For every dissatisfied coworker, there is an opportunity to create an alternative coworking space for a different community.

6.4. Evidence from Community Leaders: Manifestos and How-to Materials

Coworking community leaders provide an additional perspective on the benefits of coworking. A community leader is usually a worker him or herself but also is responsible for the success of the entire coworking community and all the workers. He or she understands the benefits of coworking, articulates these potential benefits, and works to assure that the workers in his community achieve these benefits.

The benefits described by community leaders are consistent with the studies and testimonials already discussed. These sources report that workers gain personal benefits, including satisfaction, social support, and a feeling of belonging to a community. Workers also can gain instrumental benefits, including improved productivity, skills, and networking. The community leader both offers benefits and encourages workers to help each other to benefit.

Finally, community leaders are one of the principle conduits of a broader narrative, one that situates coworking in a larger social and historical context. For many workers, coworking makes them part of a global movement that represents the future of work. For these workers, participating in this movement adds meaning to coworking and their own work.

Benefits to Workers

As discussed above, coworkers report that coworking makes them feel happy, less lonely, and a sense of belonging to a community. Coworking community leaders work to make their fellow workers happy.

One of the important goals for a coworking community leader is to try to "make peoples' lives happier" [54]. Generally, coworkers are happy because they enjoy and value the benefits of coworking, including conviviality and community. Coworking leaders recognize this and act to create and sustain social interaction and community feeling.

Community leaders create a friendly social atmosphere, personally greeting and welcoming workers and offering motivation, encouragement, and praise to fellow workers [36]. For example, Kane describes coworking as a "friendship incubator" and advises leaders, *"If you do just one thing: Say 'Welcome! I'm so glad you're here'"* [32]. Surman practices radical hospitality to create social spaces that are "warm, welcoming, and buzzing with activity" [54] "just by talking, connecting, recommending, and caring in their daily work" [41]. Kwiatkowski and Buczynski say the leader is "a daily fixture in the community" ([35], p. 14). Rachael Gursky teaches community leaders to "create an atmosphere that makes our members feel excited to come to work" [1].

A second critical responsibility of a coworking community leader is to help create a community of workers through introductions and steering collaborative and cooperative activities. Leaders aim to foster spontaneous interactions, collaboration, mutual help, and creativity (e.g., [47, 41, 52, 5] all give similar descriptions of a successful community). This means that it is important to encourage workers to actively participate in the community [24, 5, 52], which will "become your tribe, your family, and your constant support system" [36].

Coworking community leaders have created programs such as Cotivation [5] and Hoffice [25, 26] which formalize these leadership and collaborative practices. The Cotivation program forms groups who meet weekly to offer mutual support and a sense of belonging [5]. In the Cotivation group, workers give each other motivation and encouragement. Similarly, a HOffice session offers friendly encouragement and motivation through sharing goals and celebrating accomplishments at the end of the day [25, 26].

Benefits to Work and Performance

Community leaders also help the workers improve their work practices and performance, "helping members take their businesses to the next level" (quote from a job description for NextSpace from March 2016 [46]). Leaders give personal encouragement and advice to individual workers, connect workers to each other and to resources, and organize training and other events. These activities foster productivity, collaboration, and new business opportunities.

For example, Merkel says the community leader strives to "animate and stimulate interaction and collaboration among coworkers," "initiate events and regular meetings," and "get members in the coworking spirit" [41]. Surman says the leader introduces members to each other to "reveal the assets in the ecosystem" and also organizes training, mentorship, and other resources [54]. Kwiatkowski and Buczynski say the leader provides accountability, feedback, networking, collaboration, and business opportunities [36].

As discussed above, the Cotivation program encapsulates the type of benefits provided by coworking communities. In addition to social support, a Cotivation group teaches and encourages positive work behavior such as "much-needed external accountability" and "valuable feedback from a diverse group of peers" [5]. A HOffice session provides similar accountability and feedback [65]. These interactions with the community of leaders and peers improve productivity and may lead to collaborations and business opportunities.

The Big Picture

In addition to their roles as host, educator, and exemplar, coworking community leaders have one more important function: many leaders articulate a bigger picture, a narrative that situates each coworker as part of a planet-wide movement. Coworking is not really about office space, the story goes; it is a positive response to the demands of the twenty-first century economy. Each worker is not just working alone; he or she is participating in this global community and movement and creating the economy of the future [22, 37, 47]. By participating in their local coworking community, workers and the work they do are imbued with enormous significance for workers, society, and the world economy.

This narrative is told by workers themselves and, most importantly, by community leaders. For example, Surman says community leaders "embed [the workers'] activity in narratives and stories" which "translates coworking values into the space" [41]. Kwiatkowski and Buczynski say the leader helps the worker "examine the larger context of what they're doing in the world" [35]. Merkel puts it that the community leader "spin[s] stories and new meanings from their own activity, the coworkers and the specific space" ([41], p. 132).

This narrative has been articulated by the "open coworking movement" [49] and its *Coworking Manifesto* [59]. According to the *Coworking Manifesto*, coworkers are not only happier and more productive, they are participants in "a new economic engine" who are "creating an economy of innovation and creativity in our communities and worldwide" [59]. The manifesto and movement have influenced many coworkers and community leaders.

Caveats

Coworking leaders articulate a consistent description of the benefits of coworking, which influences the expectations and statements of workers and the results of surveys. But it is important to consider that this consensus partly represents successful advocacy and organization by community leaders.

Coworking leaders themselves are not disinterested observers; they are proponents of coworking, inclined to see the most favorable results and to report the most positive aspects of coworking. Most coworking leaders are personally committed to coworking and believe it is good for workers. Many strongly believe that coworking is an important contribution to the economy and the future of work.

Furthermore, coworking leaders are highly networked, often participating in an informal "community of community builders" [40], interacting with other coworking leaders digitally, in person, and at conferences (such as [22]). Through these interactions, leaders exchange and rehearse what has become their common story. An indication of this tendency is the *Coworking Manifesto,* which has been copied by many coworking sites as a description of the ideals for the local community, often without acknowledgement of the original source.

It is also important to note that coworking leaders strongly influence studies of coworking. Leaders not only teach workers what to say about coworking, but in many cases, these committed leaders are respondents in the surveys. Some surveys have been done by or in cooperation with the leadership of coworking spaces. In short, the sources discussed in this chapter cannot be taken as completely independent of each other.

That said, it is clear that coworking leaders are close observers of coworking and generally try to give honest and accurate reports. Taking all the evidence together, there seems to be a clear picture of the potential benefits of coworking.

6.5. Summary: How Well Does Coworking Work?

There is widespread evidence that coworking is good for workers, at least when the space and community match the worker's preferences. There are two major kinds of benefits for individual workers: personal and instrumental. These benefits are described in similar terms by survey data, anecdotes from workers themselves, and by community leaders who are responsible for delivering these benefits.

The benefits can be summarized briefly. Coworkers are happier and less lonely, and coworkers collaborate and help each other. Many coworkers feel and value a sense of belonging to a community of peers. Some coworkers also find an identity as part of a global community and movement.

The sources cited in this chapter are imperfect, yet there is remarkable consistency among them, which suggests that there is probably a core of truth within them. Earlier sections noted a number of caveats and limitations in these sources, particularly the fact that the bulk of the evidence is based on unrepresentative samples of workers and community leaders. In general, the information comes from workers who are *currently coworking* and who, for the most part, are highly satisfied with coworking. Thus, the data collection is clearly biased in favor of happy coworkers.

Chapter 7 considers the limits of these studies, and what conclusions can be drawn from them.

Appendix: Sources Used

Source	Notes
Surveys	
Deskmag Surveys (2010–2017) [15, 14, 13, 12, 11, 16, 53, 18, 17, 8, 9] from *Deskmag* magazine [7] and Emergent Systems [10]	Interviews and web surveys; each year has more than 1,000 respondents from around the world each year. "PARTICIPANTS OF THE SURVEY: 2011–12: 913, 2012–13: 1206, 2013–14: 1270, 2015–16: 1679, 2016–17: 1876" [9]
Gerdenitsch, C., T. E Scheel, J. Andorfer, and C. Korunka, *Coworking Spaces: A Source of Social Support for Independent Professionals* (2016) [21]	Two surveys, 69 coworkers in Austria, *154 coworkers and 609 employees in "traditional office settings"* from several parts of Europe
Spreitzer, G., P. Bacevice, and L. Garrett, *Why People Thrive in Coworking Spaces. Studies* [55, 52, 20]	An ongoing Internet survey augmented by interviews with coworking space operators by University of Michigan Coworking Project. Sample size and characteristics are not reported
Van de Vrande, V., and M. Tempelaar, "Creating Communities of Innovation" (2015) [63]	A survey of several hundred members of Seats2Meet [50] sites in the Netherlands
Fuzi, A., N. Clifton, and G. H. Loudon, *New spaces for supporting entrepreneurship? Co-working spaces in the Welsh entrepreneurial landscape"* (2015) [19].	Interviews of 46 coworkers at several different coworking communities in Wales
Klaas, Z. R., *"Coworking and Connectivity in Berlin" (2014)* [34]	A study of coworking and coworking spaces in Berlin with nine interviews and participant observation
Spinuzzi, C. "Working Alone Together: Coworking as Emergent Collaborative Activity" (2013) [51].	Interviews coworking space operators, coworkers, and examination of related written materials, from several coworking spaces in the Austin area circa 2009
Hurry, C. J. P., "The Hub Halifax : a qualitative study on coworking"	A student thesis reporting qualitative analysis of a single coworking site

(2012) [27]	(the Hub) in Halifax Nova Scotia
Tonya Surman, *several reports from* The Centre for Social Innovation (CSI) in Toronto (2016) [54, 56, 58, 57].	Includes results of a survey of 80 members
M. Janet, "Coworking in the city" (2015) [41]	Semi-structured interviews of 25 coworking hosts in Berlin, London, and New York from 2012
Anecdotes (Collections)	
Kwiatkowski, A., and B. Buczynski, *Coworking: How Freelancers Escape the Coffee Shop Office and Tales of Community from Independents around the World* (2011) [36]	Brief statements from 30 happy coworkers
Jones, D., T. Sundsted, and T. Bacigalupo, *I'm Outta Here: How Coworking Is Making the Office Obsolete* (2009) [31]	Statements from a dozen workers
King, S., *Voices of Coworking* (2011) [33]	Statements from a dozen workers
Marshall, F. A., and J. M. Witman, *Humantics: The Science and Design of Sustainable Collaboration* (2010) [39]	Interviews with 4 workers and participant observation Indy Hall coworking in Philadelphia
Wetstein, Jonathan P., *Leadership Practices of Indy Hall's Coworking Initiative (2010)* [64]	Interviews with two workers and participant observation Indy Hall coworking in Philadelphia
Anecdotes (Individual)	
Mesku, M., (2015–2016) [44, 43, 42]	Several articles about coworking experience
Johnson, C. "Look Out, Coworking. Here Comes Big Money [30]	Compares "commodity" coworking with her preferred "home" coworking community
Cropcho, J. "Coworking in NYC using Croissant" (2016) [6]	Dislikes socializing
Bhagwandin, S. "The sustainability of luxury coworking spaces" [3]	Criticizes "luxury" coworking, complains that "fun" is "distracting"
Kane, L. "Reimagination Stations: Creating a Game-Changing In-Home Coworking Space" (2015)	Describes coworking spaces that don't resemble the neighborhood outside the doors; also describes

[32] (and quoted in [29])	experience with home coworking
How-to Manuals and Manifestos	
The Coworking Manifesto [59]	A key document from the "open coworking movement," widely copied with and without attribution
The Cotivation Program, created by Tony Bacigalupo and Susan Dorsch [28, 5]	An organized program that creates weekly support groups of coworkers
Bacigalupo, T. *No More Sink Full of Mugs*. (2015) [2], also frequent blogger and curator of "open coworking" [49]	Experiences at New Work City coworking and ongoing advocacy and teaching
Surman, T., *Building Social Entrepreneurship through the Power of Coworking* (2013) [54] (also other reports and training materials, e.g., [56, 58, 57])	Experiences at The Centre for Social Innovation (CSI) in Toronto
Liquid Talent Agency. *Dude, Where's My Drone: The Future of Work and What You Can Do to Prepare for It* (2015) [37]	Describes WeWork coworking
Olma, S. *The Serendipity Machine: A Disruptive Business Model for Society 3.0* (2012) [47]	Describes Seets2Meet coworking
Kwiatkowski, A., and B. Buczynski. *"Coworking: Building Community as a Space Catalyst" (2011)* [35] as well as several how-to books, articles and videos, e.g., [36, 4]	How to be a community leader.
Gradin Franzén and Lindholm on HOffice [25, 26, 65]	Description of HOffice process, how to do a session
Kane, L. *Reimagination Stations: Creating a Game-Changing In-Home Coworking Space (2015)* [32] (and quoted in [29])	How to set up and run home coworking

Chapter References

1. Amador, Cecilia. 2016. "Learn About Hospitality from the Operator that Got it Right." *AllWork*, April 6. https://allwork.space/2016/04/learn-about-hospitality-from-the-operator-that-got-it-right/
2. Bacigalupo, Tony. 2015. "No More Sink Full of Mugs." New York: No More Sink Full of Mugs. https://sellfy.com/p/IBtB/ (accessed January, 2018).
3. Bhagwandin, Stefan. 2016. The sustainability of luxury coworking spaces. *New Worker Magazine*. Accessed January, 2018. http://newworker.co/mag/the-sustainability-of-luxury-coworking-spaces/
4. Buczynski, Beth. 2011. What Coworking Brings To The Community Table. *Sharable*. Accessed January, 2018. http://www.shareable.net/blog/what-coworking-brings-to-the-community-table
5. Cotivation. 2017
. "Cotivation - Collaborative motivation groups for coworking spaces", accessed January, 2018. http://cotivation.co/
6. Cropcho, James. 2016. "Coworking in NYC using Croissant." *New Worker Magazine*, March 6 http://newworker.co/mag/coworking-in-nyc-using-croissant/.
7. Deskmag. 2016. "Deskmag: The Coworking Magazine", accessed January, 2018. http://www.deskmag.com/
8. Deskmag. 2017. The 2017 Global Coworking Survey. Accessed January, 2018. http://www.deskmag.com/en/background-of-the-2017-global-coworking-survey
9. Deskmag. 2017. "The Global Coworking Survey." Global Coworking Unconference Conferences (GCUC), New York, May http://usa.gcuc.co/wp-content/uploads/2017/05/GCUC-2017-Global-Coworking-Survey.pdf
10. Emergent Research. 2016. "Emergent Research Tracking the Future of Small Business", accessed January, 2018. http://www.emergentresearch.com/
11. Foertsch, Carsten. 2010. Why Coworkers like their Coworking Spaces. *Deskmag*. Accessed January, 2018. http://www.deskmag.com/en/why-coworkers-like-their-coworking-spaces-162
12. Foertsch, Carsten. 2011. First results of Global Coworking Survey. *Deskmag*. Accessed January, 2018. http://www.deskmag.com/en/first-results-of-global-coworking-survey-171

13. Foertsch, Carsten. 2012. 1st Results of the 3rd Global Coworking Survey. *Deskmag*. Accessed January, 2018. http://www.deskmag.com/en/1st-results-of-the-3rd-global-coworking-survey-2012

14. Foertsch, Carsten. 2014. The Coworking Forecast 2014. *Deskmag*. Accessed January, 2018. http://www.deskmag.com/en/the-coworking-market-report-forecast-2014

15. Foertsch, Carsten. 2015. First Results Of The New Global Coworking Survey. *Deskmag*. Accessed January, 2018. http://www.deskmag.com/en/first-results-of-the-new-global-coworking-survey-2015-16

16. Foertsch, Carsten. 2016. "Results of the Global Coworking Survey." Global Coworking Unconference Conference, Los Angeles, May 4. http://canada.gcuc.co/wp-content/uploads/2016/presentations/DESKMAG%20GCUC%20GLOBAL%20COWORKING%20SURVEY%20PRESENTATION%202016%20SLIDES.pdf

17. Foertsch, Carsten. 2017. How profitable are coworking spaces today? *Deskmag*. Accessed January, 2018. http://www.deskmag.com/en/how-profitable-are-coworking-spaces-profitability-business-stats-statistics-make-money-965

18. Foertsch, Carsten. 2017. More than one million people will work in coworking spaces in 2017. *Deskmag*. Accessed January, 2018. http://www.deskmag.com/en/the-complete-2017-coworking-forecast-more-than-one-million-people-work-from-14000-coworking-spaces-s

19. Fuzi, Anita, Nick Clifton, and Gareth H. Loudon. 2015. "New spaces for supporting entrepreneurship? Co-working spaces in the Welsh entrepreneurial landscape." 8th International Conference of entrepreneurship, innovation and regional development, , Sheffield, UK, June 18-19. http://hdl.handle.net/10369/7478

20. Garrett, Lyndon Earl, Gretchen M. Spreitzer, and Peter Bacevice. 2014. "Co-constructing a Sense of Community at Work: The Emergence of Community in Coworking Spaces." *Academy of Management Proceedings* 2014 (1). doi: 10.5465/ambpp.2014.139. http://proceedings.aom.org/content/2014/1/14004.abstract

21. Gerdenitsch, Cornelia, Tabea E Scheel, Julia Andorfer, and Christian Korunka. 2016. "Coworking Spaces: A Source of Social Support for Independent Professionals." *Frontiers in psychology* 7:581. https://www.ncbi.nlm.nih.gov/pmc/articles/PMC4843169/

22. Global Coworking Unconference Conferences (GCUC) 2018. "Global Coworking Unconference Conferences (GCUC) ", accessed January, 2018. http://gcuc.co/

23. HeraHub. 2017. "Hera Hub: Workspace for Women", accessed January 2015. http://herahub.com/

24. Hillman, Alex. 2014. "To build a strong community, stop "community managing", be a Tummler instead." *Alex Hillman*, April 20. http://dangerouslyawesome.com/2014/04/community-management-tummling-a-tale-of-two-mindsets/

25. Hoffice. 2017. "Hoffice: Come and work at someone's home", accessed January, 2018. http://hoffice.nu/en/

26. Hoffice. 2017. "Hosting & Facilitating", accessed January, 2018. http://hoffice.nu/en/hosting-facilitating/

27. Hurry, Christopher J. P. 2012. "The Hub Halifax : a qualitative study on coworking." Masters of Business Administration Major Research Project, Business Administartion, St. Mary's University.

28. Johnson, Cat. 2015. Cotivation Helps Freelancers Succeed Through Mutual Accountability. *Shareable*. Accessed January, 2018. http://www.shareable.net/blog/cotivation-helps-freelancers-succeed-through-mutual-accountability

29. Johnson, Cat. 2015. The Top 10 Tips For Running a Coworking Space at Home. *Shareable*. Accessed January, 2018. http://www.shareable.net/blog/the-top-10-tips-for-running-a-coworking-space-at-home

30. Johnson, Cat. 2016. Look Out, Coworking. Here Comes Big Money. *Shareable*. Accessed January, 2018. http://www.shareable.net/blog/look-out-coworking-here-comes-big-money

31. Jones, Drew, Todd Sundsted, and Tony Bacigalupo. 2009. *I'm Outta Here: How coworking is making the office obsolete*. Austin: Not an MBA Press.

32. Kane, Lori, Tabitha Borchardt, and Bas de Baar. 2015. *Reimagination Stations: Creating a Game-Changing In-Home Coworking Space*: Lori Kane.

33. King, Steve. 2011. Voices of Coworking. https://youtu.be/QtyTUNqc_Pk.

34. Klaas, Zachary R. 2014. Coworking & Connectivity in Berlin. University of Illinois at Urbana Champaign https://www.academia.edu/11486279/Coworking_Connectivity.

35. Kwiatkowski, Angel, and Beth Buczynski. 2011. "Coworking: Building Community as a Space Catalyst." Ft. Collins: Cohere Coworking.

http://coherecommunity.com/shop/coworking-building-community-as-a-space-catalyst (accessed January, 2018).

36. Kwiatkowski, Angel, and Beth Buczynski. 2011. "Coworking: How freelancers escape the coffee shop office and tales of community from independents around the world." Fort Collins: Cohere. http://coherecommunity.com/shop/coworkers (accessed January, 2018).

37. Liquid Talent. 2015. "Dude, Where's My Drone: The future of work and what you can do to prepare for it." https://www.dropbox.com/s/405kr9keucv97gw/LiquidTalentFoWE book.pdf?dl=0 (accessed January, 2018).

38. Lynn, Samara. 2016. "Finding the Perfect Co-working Space." *Black Enterprise* 46 (9):58-59

39. Marshall, Fraser A., and Justin M. Witman. 2010. "Humantics: The Science and Design of Sustainable Collaboration." Master of Industrial Design Industrial Design Program, The University of the Arts

40. McLaren, Diana. 2015. Australian Coworking Event a Window into Growing Movement. *Shareable*. Accessed January, 2018. http://www.shareable.net/blog/australian-coworking-event-a-window-into-growing-movement

41. Merkel, Janet. 2015. "Coworking in the city." *Ephemera* 15 (1):121

42. Mesku, Melissa. 2015. Coworking: the best place for hookups in 2015? *The New Worker*. Accessed January, 2018. http://newworker.co/mag/coworking-dating-hookup/

43. Mesku, Melissa. 2016. Community: the key thing. *New Worker Magazine*. Accessed January, 2018. http://newworker.co/mag/what-your-key-says-about-your-coworking-space/

44. Mesku, Melissa. 2016. Quantifying serendipity. *New Worker Magazine*. Accessed January, 2018. http://newworker.co/mag/quantifying-serendipity-in-coworking/

45. Nebula. 2017. "Nebula Coworking St. Louis", accessed January, 2018. https://nebulastl.com/

46. NextSpace. 2017. "Careers At NextSpace", accessed March, 2016. http://nextspace.us/careers

47. Olma, Sebastian. 2012. "The Serendipity Machine: A Disruptive Business Model for Society 3.0." https://www.seats2meet.com/downloads/The_Serendipity_Machine.pdf (accessed January 2018).

48. One Roof. 2017. "One Roof", accessed January, 2018.]http://www.oneroofwomen.com/

49. Open Coworking. 2016. "Open Coworking - Building the movement together", accessed January, 2018. http://opencoworking.org/

50. Seats2Meet. 2016. "Seats2Meet - Connecting and empowering you to excel", accessed January, 2018. https://www.seats2meet.com/en

51. Spinuzzi, Clay. 2012. "Working Alone Together: Coworking as Emergent Collaborative Activity." *Journal of Business and Technical Communication* 26 (4):399-441. doi: 10.1177/1050651912444070. http://jbt.sagepub.com/content/26/4/399.abstract

52. Spreitzer, Gretchen, Peter Bacevice, and Lyndon Garrett. 2015. "Why People Thrive in Coworking Spaces." *Harvard Business Review* 93 (8):1-7. https://hbr.org/2015/05/why-people-thrive-in-coworking-spaces

53. Steve. 2015. "Coworking Spaces are Human Spaces." *Small Business Labs*, May 12. http://www.smallbizlabs.com/2015/05/coworking-spaces-are-human-spaces.html

54. Surman, Tonya. 2013. "Building Social Entrepreneurship through the Power of Coworking." *Innovations: Technology, Governance, Globalization* 8 (3-4):189-195. doi: 10.1162/INOV_a_00195. http://dx.doi.org/10.1162/INOV_a_00195

55. The Center for Positive Organizations. 2016. "University of Michigan Coworking Project", accessed May, 2016. https://ctools.umich.edu/access/content/group/26e1cf0a-9db8-45cb-9a22-92365294579f/index.html

56. The Centre for Social Innovation. 2016. "Culture | The Centre for Social Innovation", accessed January, 2018. https://socialinnovation.org/culture/

57. The Centre for Social Innovation. 2016. Proof: How Shared Spaces are Changing the World. http://socialinnovation.ca/sites/socialinnovation.ca/files/Proof_How_shared_spaces_are_changing_the_world_.pdf.

58. The Centre for Social Innovation. 2016. Rigour: How-To Create World-Changing Spaces. http://socialinnovation.ca/sites/socialinnovation.ca/files/Rigour_How_to_create_World-Changing_Shared_Spaces_.pdf.

59. The Coworking Wiki. 2015. "Coworking Manifesto (global - for the world) " *The Coworking Wiki*. http://wiki.coworking.org/w/page/35382594/Coworking%20Manifesto%20%28global%20-%20for%20the%20world%29

60. The Shift. 2017. "The Shift - Home", accessed January, 2018. http://www.theshiftchicago.com/

61. The Wing. 2017. "The Wing", accessed January, 2018. https://www.the-wing.com/

62. Thrive. 2017. "Welcome Home", accessed January, 2018. https://www.thriveaz.com/

63. Van de Vrande, Vareska, and Michiel Tempelaar. 2015. Creating Communities of Innovation. Rotterdam: Rotterdam School of Management, Erasmus University http://api.rsm.nl/files/index/get/id/1aabed80-8ebb-11e5-8275-c1f4f8ce46f7.

64. Wetstein, Jonathan P. 2010. Leadership Practices of Indy Hall's Coworking Initiative. Philadelphia: The University of the Arts Master of Industrial Design Program https://dl.dropboxusercontent.com/u/628073/IHResearch/Wetstein_IndyHall_Research.pdf.

65. Wolf, Andeas. 2016. How to "Hoffice" with Other Freelancers for More Health, Happiness and Productivity. *Sharable.* Accessed January, 2018. http://www.shareable.net/blog/how-to-hoffice-with-other-freelancers-for-more-health-happiness-and-productivity

66. Women's Business Incubator. 2016. "Women's Business Incubator", accessed March 18, 2016. http://womensincubator.org/

Chapter 7: Why Does It Work? Interpreting the Evidence

Chapter 6 presented evidence from a number of studies that indicates that workers both like coworking and believe that they benefit from it. This chapter turns to the question of how to pull together and evaluate this evidence to try to answer the questions "What do these findings mean?" and "What conclusions can be drawn from them?"

This chapter will approach these questions using several perspectives drawn from social and psychological research. These perspectives suggest alternative views of the evidence and even the definition of coworking. Taken together, these ideas give a more complete understanding of coworking and coworkers.

The first section briefly summarizes the key findings from chapter 6 that will be discussed throughout the chapter. First, workers are very satisfied with coworking. Second, workers report a variety of benefits for their work and life. In addition, there are also some workers who express dissatisfaction with coworking for a number of reasons.

There are many questions that could be asked about these findings. This chapter will focus on two big questions:

1. Are the reported benefits real?
2. Assuming the results are valid, why are coworkers so happy and coworking so beneficial?

The following sections will consider four hypotheses that offer alternative interpretations of the studies and perspectives on the future of coworking. The perspectives are

1. the data is valid, and it shows that coworking is the future of work;
2. the research is poorly designed and therefore difficult to draw conclusions from;
3. the sampling is biased, and specifically, the respondents are selected for happiness; and
4. coworking can be viewed as participatory theater.

These viewpoints are not necessarily mutually exclusive; each of them might be partially true.

7.1. What Needs to Be Explained

Earlier chapters have described coworking and its benefits for workers and their work (Table 7.1). The benefits to coworkers themselves include satisfaction, social support, and a feeling of belonging to a community. The studies also suggest that workers also produce better work, including improved productivity, collaboration with other workers, and more business opportunities.

Table 7.1 Summary of Benefits of Coworking (repeated from Chapter 6)

Benefits to Workers	
	Satisfaction (happiness)
	Social support (Relief from isolation and loneliness, friendship)
	Feeling of belonging to a community
Benefits to their work and performance	
	Improved productivity, better work, new skills
	Collaboration and creativity
	Business opportunities

Are the Reported Benefits Real?

First, are the reported benefits real? Is the evidence valid? What inferences can be drawn from it? Can the results be generalized beyond the individual studies to other workers and coworking spaces? Will the benefits persist into the future?

It is worth considering the limitations of the evidence. How strong is the methodology? Are the samples representative, and what are they representative of? What are the comparison cases?

Assuming that the results are valid, what inferences can be drawn from them? Can the findings be extrapolated to all workers and all coworking spaces? Will the effects be the same in the future?

Why Are Coworkers So Happy About Coworking? What Are Coworkers Happy About?

Second, assuming the results are valid, why are coworkers so happy? What are workers so happy (or unhappy) about? What creates the benefits of coworking?

Can we conclude that coworking is good for all workers? What are the long-term effects of coworking? Do the benefits continue for a long time, or is coworking a short-term phase in a worker's career?

7.2. Interpreting the Evidence: Some Theoretical Explanations

This chapter presents four perspectives to interpret and explain the evidence discussed in chapter 6. This approach is patterned after descriptive social science, such as an anthropologist or social psychologist might produce. Each perspective is presented as a hypothesis that strives to create a coherent viewpoint that explains the evidence and leads to general conclusions about it. In each case, there is a definition of what coworking is and what is most important about it.

As is often the case in social science, these alternative perspectives are based on quite different assumptions and emphases. Each view evaluates the data in its own way and suggests possible conclusions and implications for the future. In some cases, the explanation raises questions that cannot yet be answered. These alternative views are not necessarily mutually exclusive. Each offers potentially valuable insight into what is important and interesting about coworking. Together, they give a broader and deeper understanding of coworking, coworkers, and coworking communities.

The discussion in this chapter is informal but draws on academic research in several ways.

First, social science offers a deep understanding of how to critically evaluate the methods used in each study and how to assess the validity of the findings and assess what inferences may be drawn from them. It is particularly important to be cautious about drawing general conclusions from studies based on limited samples and also to evaluate the specific measurements used.

Second, coworking and coworking communities can be related to other social situations and phenomena, including, for example, other types of workplace or online peer-to-peer communities. Making these connections and analogies is interesting for its own sake because it helps place coworking in a historical, economic, and cultural context. In addition, analogies to other situations suggests that additional conclusions and hypotheses developed in other research may be applied to coworking, coworkers, and coworking communities, at least provisionally.

7.3. Hypothesis 1: Coworking Is the Future of Work

Conventional wisdom and the party line of both the coworking movement [34, 15] and the corporate coworking industry (e.g., as represented by the Global Coworking Unconference [15] and others [21, 18]) is that coworking is ideally suited to the new economy. The basic conclusion is that independent workers like coworking because it fits their needs so well, in several ways. From this perspective, coworking works well because it makes good use of the technology and the entrepreneurial spirit of the digital economy and also produces real psychological and economic benefits to the workers and the whole economy.

In this view, coworking is a successful match for the needs of contemporary workers and their work in two ways. First, coworking is both enabled and inspired by the technology and culture of the Internet. Second, coworking matches the needs of workers and companies in the gig economy.

Digital technology has freed work and collaboration from physical propinquity. The Internet makes it possible for workers to work anywhere and with anyone. These technical advances mean that conventional organizations and offices are no longer essential or desired by all workers. Furthermore, workers are familiar with the cultural norms and practices of the Internet, which encourage peer-to-peer social networking, collaboration, and sharing. For example, open-source development is a model for how workers thrive by contributing to group projects and products that matter to them. Crowdsourced expertise and online job markets are models for serendipity and just-in-time collaboration.

At the same time, employers increasingly embrace a piecework gig economy, eliminating long-term employment and permanent work teams. In this new way of work, production is achieved by just-in-time hiring of freelance workers who bring their own devices and have no fixed office or workplace [22, 13]. These workers need generic, on-demand office space and infrastructure. A coworking space is a perfect place to make the new way of work happen.

In addition to infrastructure, coworking offers a second important benefit for independent workers: a coworking community offers social support that independent workers want and need. A coworking space offers physical, face-to-face interactions with peers, which is both a "respite from our isolation" (a la [17]) and may also provide opportunities for personal and professional success. It is an ideal situation for mutual help, social networking, discovering new collaborations, and a creative exchange of ideas ("serendipity," a la [21]).

In short, coworkers are happy because their coworking community offers crucial social support similar to that which ideally would be found in a conventional organization and workplace.

From this perspective, coworking is closely related to digital work and digitally augmented spaces of many kinds. The large coworking chain WeWork has been characterized as a social network in a physical space. Coworking is just one of an array of similar workplaces, all of which bring communities of likeminded workers together face-to-face, generating and exploiting social capital that are the greatest value in the contemporary economy. For example, maker spaces and business incubators have similar technological and social features, as do some corporate design labs.

7.4. Hypothesis 2: The Research Methods Are Questionable

An alternative hypothesis is that much of the evidence is based on weak studies with poor research methods. Consequently, it is difficult to draw conclusions about coworking and coworkers from these studies.

The evidence reported in chapter 6 comes mostly from personal testimony (self-reported anecdotal data). While the workers and community leaders are no doubt honest and well intentioned, they are scarcely disinterested or completely objective and certainly have limited knowledge.

Self-reported data has many well-known pitfalls. These include

- psychological biases, including desire for approval and ego defense;
- limited perspective and personal filtering; and
- effects of social influence, including group think and cultural biases.

It is worth noting the wide influence of the early coworking movement. The *Coworking Manifesto* has been widely disseminated and is often echoed (with and without attribution) by many people and organizations. The ideas stated in the *Coworking Manifesto* are generally reflected throughout the testimony and surveys reported in chapter 6. This probably indicates that workers and leaders have been taught what coworking *should* be and have found or made it so.

The surveys and interviews discussed in chapter 6 also suffer from ambiguous and poorly phrased questions. For example, a number of studies have asked workers some variant of the question, "How happy are you?" Personal happiness is a subjective and individual value and is highly dependent on history and context. Are all "happy" workers happy in the same degree or the same way? The large annual survey reported at GCUC reports that workers are "happier" coworking. This begs the question, "Happier than what?" Are all workers comparing coworking to the same alternatives?

Other key findings raise similar questions. Workers report that they are "more productive" when coworking. They also report successful social networking, collaboration, and business opportunities. Again, an important question is whether all workers are thinking about productivity and success in the same way.

These challenges are exacerbated by the diversity of coworking spaces, communities, and workers. A given worker has experience with one or a handful of workplaces. There are many different communities of likeminded peers, so the reports indicate that some workers are satisfied with some coworking spaces. This does not mean that any given coworking space will suit all workers or that a given worker would be satisfied with other coworking spaces.

The overall question is how should these reports be interpreted? What conclusions can be drawn about coworking in general?

Is coworking better than other work arrangements?

It seems clear that workers are happy and productive in a coworking space mainly in comparison to working alone. However, many workers leave their coworking space to take up conventional employment. Satisfaction with coworking may be a case of making the best of what you can get.

Is coworking good for all workers?

The fact that some workers are satisfied and successful in their current coworking space does not imply that other workers will be equally satisfied and successful in that space or any other coworking space.

Is coworking a long-term career?

Similarly, the fact that a given worker is satisfied and successful now does not imply that even this same worker will continue to be happy coworking. Indeed, most coworkers seem to leave the community within a year or two. Furthermore, many of the departing workers go to conventional offices as permanent employees or to run their own new business. For these workers, coworking is a valuable but temporary phase in their career, left behind for better work environments.

7.5. Hypothesis 3: The Samples Are Biased

The anecdotes and surveys so-far discussed also suffer from a variety of forms of poor sampling: they do not necessarily represent the overall population of workers and workplaces.

Overall, the studies do not use any form of representative sampling at all. Many studies sample a few workers at one or a few convenient local workplaces. The largest surveys (the Michigan study [30] and the *Deskmag* surveys [9, 8, 7, 6, 5, 10, 31, 12, 11, 2, 3]) are web surveys, which are entirely self-selected (i.e., the respondents choose to participate). It is difficult to say how representative of all coworkers the samples are.

One problem in all the studies is that there are no common definitions of coworking. What is a coworking space? Who is a coworker? Without firm definitions, it isn't possible to define what a representative sample would even be.

For example, the notion of "membership" in a coworking space is not a clear-cut or well-defined concept. Some coworking operations have formal membership (e.g., workers with a paid subscriptions), while others are open to anyone. Even when membership is formally defined, there are a great variety of arrangements, ranging from hour by hour through long-term rental. In addition, some workers work every day (possibly twenty-four hours a day), others work one day per week, and others work sporadically according to project demands. Some workers patronize the same workplace for years; others spend only a day or two before moving on. The latter workers also include digital nomads, who have no fixed abode and tenuous connection to any particular coworking community.

A given coworking community may have members with any and all of these levels of commitment, as well as frequent collaborators who are not formally members at all. Who of these workers should count as a "current coworker"?

In the absence of better alternatives, studies and reports generally include workers who self-identify members of a self-identified coworking space or community. Each study has at least slightly different criteria to define these concepts, which means that the different studies may not be comparable to each other.

This pervasive self-selection suggests that these studies may well suffer from a form of *survivor bias*. Survivor bias is a common logical fallacy that retroactively infers causality from the characteristics of a sample of currently successful cases [25, 27]. For example, characteristics of a successful business are taken to be the cause of that success without considering the characteristics of similar, less successful businesses. (This fallacy is frequently seen in sales pitches and popular business literature.)

In the case of coworking, the studies of current coworkers and workplaces show that workers are satisfied and successful, and draw the inference that coworking has caused these benefits. However, many workers may have opted out, moved to more congenial workplaces, or never coworked at all and therefore were not surveyed. For that matter, unsuccessful coworking spaces cannot be sampled, either. This pattern is a classic case of survivor bias.

This bias is due in large part to the very nature of coworking itself: coworking is, by design and definition, self-selected. Unlike most conventional workplaces, coworkers choose their workplace and community of fellow workers. Workers self-select into coworking situations that make them happy and productive, and they can and do select out if they are dissatisfied. In addition, workers may choose to cowork only when and for as long as they wish to.

For that matter, happy coworkers are satisfied with a *specific* coworking space and community. There are many coworking spaces, each with its own features and community of workers. In many cities, a worker can choose among dozens of coworking spaces to find a workplace that makes them happy and productive, even if other coworking space would be unsatisfactory.

In addition, every coworking space must retain sufficient workers to stay in business. A coworking *space* that does not satisfy some workers will close and will not be sampled. Thus, every coworking space must be inhabited mostly by happy workers most of the time, or it cannot exist.

In short, the very self-selecting nature of coworking assures that any sample of current coworkers will contain mostly satisfied workers.

The most important implication is that the data must be interpreted cautiously. It seems that some workers are satisfied in some coworking spaces, some of the time. But the studies do not necessarily indicate that coworking *in general* is beneficial or satisfying or that all workers would be well served by coworking.

Leo Tolstoy wrote *"All happy families are alike; each unhappy family is unhappy in its own way"* (from Anna Karenina). Perhaps *every coworking community is happy in its own way*.

It is also important to realize that this data does not indicate whether coworking will grow or shrink in the future. Many proponents argue that the high levels of satisfaction and success mean that coworking is a model for the future of work and that more and more workers will choose to cowork. However, it is just as plausible to infer that nearly everyone who wants to cowork in current spaces is already coworking. In any case, much of the growth in coworking will depend on the ability of coworking spaces to meet the needs and preferences of workers who are *not currently happy coworkers*.

7.6. Hypothesis 4: Coworking Is Participatory Theater

The fourth perspective is rather different: consider coworking as a form of participatory theater.

The essence of this idea is to view a coworking space as the stage for an improvised, participatory play. Workers are invited to enact the role of coworker in a story about the new way of work. Like an improv theater exercise, the players (workers) make up the dialog and action for themselves within an overall storyline [24, 29].

Viewed from this perspective, a key aspect of coworking is learning and acting out a narrative about working. The basic story is set forth by many sources, including the widely endorsed *Coworking Manifesto*, which declares that

> Coworking is redefining the way we do work.
>
> We are a group of connected individuals and small businesses creating an economy of innovation and creativity in our communities and worldwide. [34]

In this epic narrative, each worker has an important and, perhaps, heroic role to play. The workspace itself is, therefore, a stage or theater set on which the performance occurs. The design and décor of the workspace is important because it is the setting and props for the play that takes place there. However, as in any play, the stage setting does not define the play itself, which is the sum of what the workers do there.

The most important implication of this perspective is that coworking is something that a group of workers do together. As Garrett *et al.* put it, workers experience a sense of community by "espousing, learning, enacting" membership in the community [14].

A coworking community generally has little or no formal social hierarchy. Coworkers consider each other to be peers. However, a successful community generally has one or more individuals who play the role of community leader, as discussed in Chapter 5. Part of the responsibility of a coworking community leader is akin to the director or facilitator of an improvisational theater workshop. The facilitator sets the scene and gives suggestions and feedback as the action progresses. "For improvisational theater, [the director's] part in the theater action is to see and select the scene or story as it emerges out of the actor's playing" ([29], p. 297).

What Is the Story?

The *Coworking Manifesto* and similar materials sketch an epic narrative, which is expressed in many local variants—that is, in the cultures or vibes of individual coworking communities. The basic story might be stated something like this:

> A group of scrappy (young) freelancers, banding together to help each other and have fun along the way.

A coworking community might adopt a variation of this, such as

> A group of scrappy (young) *business entrepreneurs* band together to help each other *disrupt the universe* and have fun along the way.

Or perhaps,

> A group of scrappy (young) *social entrepreneurs* band together to help *make the world better* and have some fun along the way.

The story might be about specific populations of workers, such as women, digital nomads, or residents of a local neighborhood. Or the story might focus on specific types of work, such as writing, media production, software development, business development, or community service.

How Does Enacting a Narrative Benefit Workers?

There are several possible ways that "enacting community" in this way could be beneficial for workers.

First, taking up a role as a "coworker" is a form of on-the-job training that is especially important for freelancers and independent contractors. When a worker joins in to play his part, he learns how to *act like* a successful worker and therefore *becomes* a more successful and happier worker. The notion is that participating in a community of peers who face similar challenges is a good way to learn. Furthermore, solo, independent workers may have few sources for learning the practice of freelancing.

Second, independent workers have considerable autonomy to work how, when, and why they want to. They may make use of this autonomy to *write the story of their own work and life.* Playing a part in a narrative is one way to frame their own work and goals, to express their personal identity.

Furthermore, participating in a coworking community is a collaborative co-creation of a group identity and, for many, playing a part in redefining work and society. This is collaborative co-creation, and gives work and life a larger, more emotionally satisfying meaning.

Relationships to Social Theory

This dramaturgical perspective links coworking to many threads of academic study. (This connection is quite visible in Garret (2014) [14] and

Spinuzzi (2012) [28], for example). Roles and role theory have been applied to understanding many social phenomena, including work (e.g., [16, 20] in [23]).

Coworking communities share many characteristics and values of participatory digital cultures, as described by Shirkey [26], Tapscott [33], and many others [35, 32, 1, 4]. For example, coworking communities typically aim to be an open and minimally hierarchical organization (often termed *peer to peer* and *open source*), with an emphasis on collaboration and knowledge exchange.

Coworking also can be viewed as akin to the co-creation that takes place in a fan community: a community of gamers, collectors, or enthusiasts. These groups of likeminded individuals identify with the group and its norms and actively participate in and co-create a partly scripted narrative. Online and in face-to-face meetings, the community networks and performs cultural rituals, tells stories, and dresses up [19, 4].

One important psychological effect of coworking for an individual worker is that by taking up the role of coworker in his community, he or she adopts and enacts the identity of coworker. He or she can say, "I *am* a coworker." This identity is particularly important for isolated independent workers living from gig to gig and who therefore do not necessarily have the social status that would be represented by a career or professional title.

Summary

Thinking about coworking as a form of participatory theater leads to a number of insights. A coworking space is the stage on which a story is acted out. Just as a play isn't just "actors talking on a stage," coworking isn't about working alone in the same room with other solo workers. It is about a group of workers playing their parts to co-create a story about the future of work.

It is important to note that this view of coworking is consistent with and derives from strong threads in social and psychological research and from observations of other contemporary "participatory cultures." For example, coworking communities have similarities to digital communities (such as open-source software communities) and fandom (such as science fiction and comic fans). This similarity suggests that observations about these communities probably apply to coworkers and coworking communities.

Studies of communities suggest that coworking probably offers psychological and social benefits to workers just as participating in other community cultures does. For instance, an otherwise isolated independent work gains status and identity as a member of a coworking group. Furthermore, participating in and co-creating this (heroic) narrative about the future of work gives the worker and their work a larger and deeper meaning.

In addition to the pleasures of face-to-face participation and co-creation, role playing is also a potentially effective training method by which solo workers develop work and relationship skills. In other words, some of the most important instrumental benefits of coworking, such as improved productivity, might well be developed through the process of learning to play the role of coworker. In addition, the generic coworking narrative itself *describes* these benefits and therefore defines the role of a coworker to be a person who learns, collaborates, and thrives.

7.7. Summary: Perspectives on Coworking

In earlier chapters, coworking was described along with evidence from many sources about purported benefits of coworking. This chapter considered how to interpret this evidence. Are the reported benefits real? If so, why are coworkers so happy and coworking so beneficial?

Four hypotheses were considered, each of which offers a different perspective and interpretation of the studies and what implications may be drawn from them. These viewpoints are not necessarily mutually exclusive; each may be partially true.

The first perspective takes conventional wisdom at face value to conclude that coworking is a perfect fit for the gig economy. This is why it works well and makes workers happy. This perspective projects that gig working and coworking might well continue to grow and displace other work environments.

The second perspective calls into question the strength of the evidence. In particular, the data is mostly self-reports or ethnographic observations and therefore subject to well-known biases and limitations. In addition, many of the concepts are poorly defined, and therefore the reports are often semantically ambiguous. For example, when a worker reports that he has achieved "improved productivity," what is he talking about, and how valid is his intuition? Taking all the reservations together, there is very little solid evidence about the purported benefits of coworking. It is difficult to project the future of coworking.

A third perspective notes that the studies are based on very limited and non-representative samples of workers and workplaces. Almost all the data is from workers who are currently coworking—that is, current members of active coworking spaces and communities. The data indicates that these workers are satisfied and successful in the workplace, but this is partly or largely because the samples are primarily made up of workers who are satisfied with their current coworking space.

This is a classic case of survivor bias. The coworking spaces sampled are successful at the time of the study, and the workers sampled have chosen to work in those spaces. Almost none of the data includes workers from closed coworking operations, workers who were dissatisfied and left a coworking space, or workers who have never coworked at all. From these studies and testimonies, we can only conclude from this data that some workers are happy some of the time in some coworking spaces. It isn't possible to conclude whether coworking will satisfy other workers or even whether the workers will continue to succeed or be satisfied in the future.

Finally, drawing from social and psychological theories, coworking can be viewed as a form of participatory theater. This dramaturgical perspective suggests that coworking is analogous to improvised theater, in which a group of workers co-create a narrative about contemporary work and life. Workers act out a role in this heroic story, and in the process learn to be more successful, gain an identity and social status, and enjoy the pleasures of face-to-face interaction, collaboration, and creativity.

It's Complicated?

Together, these perspectives suggest that coworking is a complicated phenomenon, with no one simple explanation. It is clear that coworking makes workers happy—at least some workers, some of the time. It is also clear that the data available to date is quite limited, and not representative of workers or workplaces in general. For this reason, it isn't possible to draw broad conclusions about the benefits or future of coworking.

One interesting idea from these perspectives is that coworking recreates the social and narrative aspect of conventional workplaces without a single organizational or management direction. Instead, as in the case of fandom and digital social media, participants opt in to the group, group identity, and social activities. In this sense, coworking might be a way for workers to gain the benefits of a congenial workplace without the overhead of a conventional organization and workplace.

Above all, though, it is important to bear in mind that coworking is a diverse phenomenon that is implemented in many small and local communities and locations. Conclusions and lessons from one time and place may or may not apply to other workers or workplaces.

Chapter References

1. Delwiche, Aaron, and Jennifer Jacobs Henderson, eds. 2013. *The Participatory Cultures Handbook*. New York: Routledge.
2. Deskmag. 2017. The 2017 Global Coworking Survey. Accessed January, 2018. http://www.deskmag.com/en/background-of-the-2017-global-coworking-survey
3. Deskmag. 2017. "The Global Coworking Survey." Global Coworking Unconference Conferences (GCUC), New York, May http://usa.gcuc.co/wp-content/uploads/2017/05/GCUC-2017-Global-Coworking-Survey.pdf
4. Duffett, Mark. 2013. *Understanding Fandom : An Introduction to the Study of Media Fan Culture*. New York: Bloomsbury.
5. Foertsch, Carsten. 2010. Why Coworkers like their Coworking Spaces. *Deskmag*. Accessed January, 2018. http://www.deskmag.com/en/why-coworkers-like-their-coworking-spaces-162
6. Foertsch, Carsten. 2011. First results of Global Coworking Survey. *Deskmag*. Accessed January, 2018. http://www.deskmag.com/en/first-results-of-global-coworking-survey-171
7. Foertsch, Carsten. 2012. 1st Results of the 3rd Global Coworking Survey. *Deskmag*. Accessed January, 2018. http://www.deskmag.com/en/1st-results-of-the-3rd-global-coworking-survey-2012
8. Foertsch, Carsten. 2014. The Coworking Forecast 2014. *Deskmag*. Accessed January, 2018. http://www.deskmag.com/en/the-coworking-market-report-forecast-2014
9. Foertsch, Carsten. 2015. First Results Of The New Global Coworking Survey. *Deskmag*. Accessed January, 2018. http://www.deskmag.com/en/first-results-of-the-new-global-coworking-survey-2015-16
10. Foertsch, Carsten. 2016. "Results of the Global Coworking Survey." Global Coworking Unconference Conference, Los Angeles, May 4. http://canada.gcuc.co/wp-content/uploads/2016/presentations/DESKMAG%20GCUC%20GLOBAL%20COWORKING%20SURVEY%20PRESENTATION%202016%20SLIDES.pdf
11. Foertsch, Carsten. 2017. How profitable are coworking spaces today? *Deskmag*. Accessed January, 2018. http://www.deskmag.com/en/how-profitable-are-coworking-spaces-profitability-business-stats-statistics-make-money-965

12. Foertsch, Carsten. 2017. More than one million people will work in coworking spaces in 2017. *Deskmag*. Accessed January, 2018. http://www.deskmag.com/en/the-complete-2017-coworking-forecast-more-than-one-million-people-work-from-14000-coworking-spaces-s

13. Freelancers Union. 2016. Freelancing in America: 2016. New York: Freelancers Union and Upwork https://fu-prod-storage.s3.amazonaws.com/content/None/FreelancinginAmerica2016report.pdf.

14. Garrett, Lyndon Earl, Gretchen M. Spreitzer, and Peter Bacevice. 2014. "Co-constructing a Sense of Community at Work: The Emergence of Community in Coworking Spaces." *Academy of Management Proceedings* 2014 (1). doi: 10.5465/ambpp.2014.139. http://proceedings.aom.org/content/2014/1/14004.abstract

15. Global Coworking Unconference Conferences (GCUC) 2018. "Global Coworking Unconference Conferences (GCUC) ", accessed January, 2018. http://gcuc.co/

16. Hindin, Michelle J. 2007. "Role Theory." In *Blackwell Encyclopedia of Sociology*, edited by George Ritzer, 2951-2954. Malden, MA: Blackwell Publishers.

17. Klaas, Zachary R. 2014. Coworking & Connectivity in Berlin. University of Illinois at Urbana Champaign https://www.academia.edu/11486279/Coworking_Connectivity.

18. Liquid Talent. 2015. "Dude, Where's My Drone: The future of work and what you can do to prepare for it." https://www.dropbox.com/s/405kr9keucv97gw/LiquidTalentFoWEbook.pdf?dl=0 (accessed January, 2018).

19. Maggs, Sam. 2015. *The Fangirl's Guide to the Galaxy: a Handbook for Geek Girls*. Philadelphia: Quirk Books.

20. Manning, Peter Kirby. 2007. "Dramaturgy." In *Blackwell Encyclopedia of Sociology*, edited by George Ritzer, 1226-1229. Malden, MA: Blackwell Publishers.

21. Olma, Sebastian. 2012. "The Serendipity Machine: A Disruptive Business Model for Society 3.0." https://www.seats2meet.com/downloads/The_Serendipity_Machine.pdf (accessed January 2018).

22. Oxford International Institute. 2016. "Introducing the iLabour Project", accessed January, 2018. http://ilabour.oii.ox.ac.uk/

23. Ritzer, George, ed. 2007. *The Blackwell Encyclopedia of Sociology*. Malden, MA: Blackwell.

24. Salinsky, Tom, and Deborah Frances-White. 2008. *The Improv Handbook: The Ultimate Guide to Improvising in Comedy, Theater,*

and Beyond. New York: Teh continuum International Publicshing Group, Inc.

25. Shermer, Michael. 2014. "Surviving Statistics." *Scientific American* 311 (3):94-94. https://www.scientificamerican.com/article/how-the-survivor-bias-distorts-reality/

26. Shirky, Clay. 2010. *Cognitive Surplus: Creativity and Generosity in a Connected Age*. New York: The Penguin Press.

27. Smith, Gary. 2014. *Standard Deviations: Flawed Assumptions, Tortured Data, and Other Ways to Lie With Statistics* New York: Overlook Duckworth.

28. Spinuzzi, Clay. 2012. "Working Alone Together: Coworking as Emergent Collaborative Activity." *Journal of Business and Technical Communication* 26 (4):399-441. doi: 10.1177/1050651912444070. http://jbt.sagepub.com/content/26/4/399.abstract

29. Spolin, Viola. 1999. *Improvisation for the Theater: A Handbook of Teaching and Directing Techniques (Third Edition)*. Evanston: Northwestern University Press.

30. Spreitzer, Gretchen, Peter Bacevice, and Lyndon Garrett. 2015. "Why People Thrive in Coworking Spaces." *Harvard Business Review* 93 (8):1-7. https://hbr.org/2015/05/why-people-thrive-in-coworking-spaces

31. Steve. 2015. "Coworking Spaces are Human Spaces." *Small Business Labs*, May 12. http://www.smallbizlabs.com/2015/05/coworking-spaces-are-human-spaces.html

32. Sunstein, Cass R. 2006. *Infotopia: How Many Minds Produce Knowledge*. New York: Oxford University Press.

33. Tapscott, Don, and Anthony D. Williams. 2006. *Wikinomics: How Mass Collaboration Changes Everything*. New York: Penguin.

34. The Coworking Wiki. 2015. "Coworking Manifesto (global - for the world) " *The Coworking Wiki*. http://wiki.coworking.org/w/page/35382594/Coworking%20Manifesto%20%28global%20-%20for%20the%20world%29

35. Zoref, Lior. 2015. *Mindsharing: The Art of Crowdsourcing Everything*. New York: Penguin.

Part IV. Coworkers of the World, Unite!

Chapter 8: The Coworking Movement

Contemporary coworking emerged early in the twenty-first century, and from the beginning it has been associated with a movement styled after the open-source movement. Many workers see coworking to be more than a convenient way to work. By coworking, they are participating in a global movement that is remaking work, the economy, and the world.

If there ever was a truly unified global coworking movement, it has become fragmented in recent years. As coworking has grown and diversified, conceptions of the coworking movement have diverged, even among the most committed leaders.

8.1. A Movement: The Community of Community Builders?

Over the last decade thousands of coworking spaces have opened every year, each of them with its own community of workers and a local culture. Many people perceive a common thread that ties all these disparate efforts together as part of a global movement. This movement advocates for the concepts of coworking, spreads best practices, and, as Diana McLaren describes it, does *"community building for the community of community builders"* [46].

The earliest history of the contemporary coworking movement is disputed but appears to have emerged in the Bay Area circa 2005. *Deskmag's* "History of Coworking" [18] suggests that the current term was coined circa 1999 by Bernard De Koven (or Brian DeKoven?), who subsequently became leader of the Coworking Institute [60]. De Koven himself traces the origins of the movement to San Francisco in 2005 [17]. On the other hand, Brad Neuberg says he invented the concept and coined the term *coworking* circa 2005 and explains the antecedents to this idea [49].

Like other movements of the Internet age, the coworking movement is loosely defined and decentralized. The coworking movement is visible in blogs, wikis, and discussion lists (e.g., [12, 65, 14, 64, 13]), as well as virtual organizations such as The Coworking Institute [60] and Open Coworking [54]. The coworking movement has at least two electronic magazines (*New Worker Magazine* [50], *Deskmag* [19]), and there are frequent conferences in every corner of the world, such as Coworking Africa [11], Coworking Europe [15], and the Global Coworking Unconference Conferences (GCUC) [26].

The coworking movement was originally patterned after the open-source movement [70] and other Internet-based sociotechnical movements such as Bitcoin [45, 55] and the maker movement [1, 20, 25]. Like open-source projects, the coworking movement is open to anyone who endorses or identifies with some broad principles and concepts, though each individual may have his or her own interpretation of the shared values.

In addition to ideas about the value and practice of open workplaces, the coworking movement is often associated with ideas about the contemporary working world. A coworking space is a place where the new economy happens, so coworking is associated with the "gig economy" [58], "the sharing economy" [44], "digital nomadism" [35, 3], and the freelancing movement [33, 23]. Furthermore, coworking spaces are seen to be a prime site for the innovation and creativity of the creative economy [22]. In fact, some view coworking as more than just a good place for independent workers, but as a key to the future of the economy [43], a sustainable planet [62], and even the lynchpin of post-capitalist "Society 3.0" [53].

Thus, the idea of the coworking movement emerged at the birth of contemporary coworking. The movement is primarily a story that recasts the otherwise mundane practice of low-cost, on-demand office rental into an exciting narrative about a new economy and society. As discussed in chapter 7, the coworking movement invites an individual worker to enact his or her own role in a worldwide story, which connects them to workers all over the planet. This participatory narrative imparts a larger meaning to work.

The original coworking movement represented a federation of small, local operations in which the owners, operators, community leaders, and workers were a single, fairly unified group. However, as the coworking has grown, the idea of a single, global coworking movement has evolved and diverged into several distinct camps. In part, this reflects the diverging interests of these stakeholders.

The great diversity of workers and local communities involved means that the experience of coworking is scarcely uniform. Even workers who endorse the general principles of the coworking movement may or may not have much in common with other coworkers or feel much solidarity with a global movement. For many workers, coworking is little more than inexpensive, on-demand infrastructure. And, of course, different workers prefer different kinds of community and social interaction.

Community leaders still embrace the coworking movement as an extension of their mission to create and foster their own community. As community leadership is becoming a profession of expert community builders, the coworking movement is *"community building for the community of community builders"* [46].

At the same time, coworking has been incorporated as part of the services of many conventional organizations, including schools, libraries, and business incubators. Some companies have adopted coworking as a form of very open office. These organizations view coworking as a better work environment, and may endorse at least some of the principles of the coworking movement, even though the workers are part of a conventional, hierarchical organization. Coworking also appears in a variety of non-work settings, such as "coliving" [69, 36], coworking resorts [67, 52, 59, 7] and "co-workations" (i.e., coworking vacations) [48]. These variations stretch the original ideas of a global coworking movement to its limits.

Coworking has also been appropriated by commercial office rental operations, which have adopted coworking practices and terminology into a new "social office industry" [9]. For some, coworking is the platform for the new economy, analogous to ubiquitous digital services that have become de facto standards used by many companies. This is a large-scale, impersonal, and uniform view of coworking, which seems very distant from the original coworking movement.

8.2. The Rhetoric of the Global Coworking Community: The Coworking Manifesto

The global coworking movement is essentially a shared story, recounted and lived out by workers and community leaders around the world. One of the most important sources for this story is the *Coworking Manifesto* [62]. The manifesto dates from roughly 2008. An early version is attributed to a collaboration of the Citizen Space in San Francisco (now a chain [6]) and the Gangplank Collective of Phoenix [24].

The manifesto has been endorsed by thousands of individuals (see [16]) and has been widely republished in the documentation of hundreds of coworking spaces around the world. This text has influenced how coworkers talk and think about coworking and helped define a global identity for otherwise isolated independent workers.

The manifesto proclaims that coworking is "the future of working," which is "a new economic engine composed of collaboration and community." The movement is placed in the context of the economic crash of the early twenty-first century, a time when "society is facing unprecedented economic, environmental, social and cultural challenges." The solution to these challenges is "new innovations." One innovation is coworking, which is a "key to turning these challenges into opportunities to improve our communities and our planet" [62].

The manifesto describes six values that define this global coworking movement. The community is inclusive, but "the member spaces of Open Coworking have all committed to some values which we all share" [63].

Community

Coworking is all about community. Hillman talks about "community first" and the necessity for "togetherness," "trust," and participation [30]. Kwiatkowski points out the importance of in-person, face-to-face interaction in addition to the ubiquitous but impersonal digital community [42].

Collaboration

Hillman says that "coworking creates opportunities for people to interact in a 'high contact' environment," which leads to creativity and serendipity [31].

Openness

This attribute is modeled after the open-source software movement [70]. However, in this context, openness mainly implies "freedom to make it whatever you want" [29]—that is, for workers to create their own communities and workplaces.

Sustainability

There are two senses of this term, and coworking claims both of them. Hillman emphasizes that sustainability means being financially self-sufficient and therefore not dependent on external funding sources [27]. Kwiatkowski makes a case that coworking is also ecologically friendly: a working space is local, efficiently shares resources, and is generally low waste [41].

Accessibility

"Open coworking" should mean that everyone should be welcomed equally [28], though generally speaking, people will self-select in or out of a particular coworking community. It is important to note that this value is not universally endorsed. Many coworking spaces are curated by operators, leaders, or the workers themselves. Other coworking spaces have fees that effectively keep out less affluent workers.

In addition to these general values, the manifesto also defines a view of the proper spirit of this global community. This is expressed in a list of desired attributes:

- collaboration over competition
- community over agendas
- participation over observation
- doing over saying
- friendship over formality
- boldness over assurance
- learning over expertise
- people over personalities
- "value ecosystem" over "value chain"

These concepts are rather hazy, but the general thrust is describing a non-hierarchical, peer-to-peer community of entrepreneurs.

The values espoused in the *Coworking Manifesto* are similar to the themes of many contemporary analyses of innovation and economic success. For example, collaboration, hands-on "doing," and continuous learning are generally seen as important for innovation [40]. The Maker movement argues for the importance of collaborative learning and doing [1, 25, 21]. In this, the *Coworking Manifesto* both appropriates many current ideas and also situates coworking as a part of this new economy.

As discussed in chapter 7, the *Coworking Manifesto* is one of the main sources of an epic story about "scrappy young entrepreneurs" who are changing the world. Independent workers are invited to join this worldwide community and advance this mission of global change. To do this, the worker will enact the role of coworker and thereby participate in the improvised theatrical performance called coworking.

8.3. The Coworking Industry and the Coming of Commodity Coworking

Historically, coworking arose partly as a rebellion against conventional corporate office environments and to foster the creative anarchy of the startup economy in Silicon Valley. Commercial office space is, to borrow the words of Melissa Mesku, "seamless and dry" [47]. Coworking communities offer conviviality, the feeling of belonging to a community, and exciting creativity that is missing from a conventional organization and workplace.

As coworking has grown and become more popular, conventional corporations have taken note of its apparent success. Some companies have begun to emulate the idea, organizing open, non-hierarchical workspaces or even placing employees in open coworking spaces. These efforts seek to create a community spirit in their workforce and to foster collaboration and creativity within a wider group of workers.

The commercial rental office industry has also taken note of the growth and popularity of coworking, as well as the opportunities to be found in fine-grained rentals (e.g., on-demand rental desks). Offering coworking space is both an attractive marketing scheme and a way to maximize occupancy and minimize expenses.

From the point of view of a company or commercial rental operation, the critical idea from coworking is that the value of a "social office" is "community [as] a product" (per [9]). Like Facebook and other social media companies, this business model is based on selling your customers—in this case, selling them to each other.

There has been a growth in networks and alliances among independent and syndicated coworking spaces. Some coworking spaces operate as chains (e.g., WeWork [68] Seats2Meet [53], NextSpace [51], and many others), and others band together in local alliances (e.g., Seattle Collaborative Space Alliance (SCSA) [57] and Chicago Deskpass [5]). There are global networks of spaces offering members access to coworking around the world (e.g., The League of Extraordinary Coworking Space [66], Coworking Pass Europe [61], Cowork Pass [10] and CoPass [8], Impact Hub [34]).

These groups offer a consistent service across many locations and membership in a large "community of communities." This offers much larger social networks than any individual coworking community, though with less intense interaction and less personal and local identification.

These developments lead some to view coworking as another ubiquitous "platform," analogous to digital peer-to-peer systems, such as Facebook or PayPal [4, 56]. In this case, ubiquitous access to coworking space is a platform for working in the gig economy [37]. Just as digital platforms such as social media, cloud services, location, and electronic markets enable people to *digitally* share, collaborate, and innovate, coworking spaces enable independent workers to share, collaborate, and innovate *in person.*

The important implication of this analogy is to search for just the right constellation of services and the optimal "interface" for the platform. In the case of coworking, the interface amounts to standardized services and contracts that will create stable and inexpensive infrastructure that workers can count on wherever and whenever they need it.

Altogether, these commercial developments see the coworking movement as a ubiquitous business platform, leading toward *commodity coworking.* For these operators, what was originally a somewhat bohemian movement modeled on open-source software has now become a segment of the "service office" or "social office" industry. The community of coworkers is both an important product and the customer base of this industry.

8.4. A Fragmented Movement?

The coworking movement appears to have fragmented into several factions, reflecting not only different philosophies but also the interests and goals of different stakeholders. Broadly speaking, the coworking movement includes three categories of stakeholders: operators, leaders, and workers.

This fragmentation was on display at the Global Coworking Unconference Conference (GCUC) in 2016. For its first few years, GCUC was a premier venue for the whole coworking community, fostering a sense of worldwide common purpose among workers, leaders, and operators. The original *Coworking Manifesto* describes the world coworking movement with the declaration "[w]e are a group of connected individuals and small businesses" who are working together to make a better world.

In a major swerve, the GCUC rebranded itself as the Global Coworking Alliance [26]. The Alliance speaks for "[w]e, the operators," who are a segment of the emerging "service office" or "social office" industry [9]. The talks focused on topics of interest to "the industry," including the potential for explosive growth, the economics of very large-scale operations, aspects of technical infrastructure, and the design of multipurpose spaces. There was, in turn, very little attention to social entrepreneurship or to work practices and community building.

Long-time observer Cat Johnson commented that the GCUC meeting "felt like it had been hijacked" [38]. Esteemed veteran coworking leader Tony Bacigalupo addressed the conference and criticized "consumer coworking" as "lame" [2]. He advocated a bottom-up, community-run coworking, which he called "authentic coworking."

Long-time coworking proponent Alex Hillman criticized the emergence of "the coworking industry" as navel gazing, commenting that "too many people in the coworking industry are spending more [sic] too much time paying attention to what's happening in the coworking 'industry.'" He argued that these conversations neglect the most important resource, the *members* of coworking communities (i.e., the workers): "'industry' conversations historically don't include the customer" [32].

Reacting to Cottle's remark that "community is a product" [9], Bacigalupo tweeted,

> "Community is a product like a soul is a body part."

A twitter exchange on the topic concluded that "'Corporate coworking' is a threat to coworking like McDonalds is a threat to the restaurant industry. (it's not)" (from [39]).

These arguments reflect different philosophies and different meanings about the definition and importance of community. The following table suggests the intertwined interests of the stakeholders.

Who	Coworking is about...
Workers	The working environment, including infrastructure the other workers in the space, and getting work done
Community leaders	Creating and sustaining a thriving community culture and helping workers succeed
Operators	Filling seats, optimizing resource use

These interests obviously overlap because everyone wants to have a thriving community of successful workers. Also, these are scarcely mutually exclusive goals, because an individual may play any or all of these roles simultaneously or at different times over his or her career.

However, these different goals are an underlying reason for the split in the coworking movement between "consumer coworking" and "authentic coworking." The former is primarily a perspective of operators, who seek to optimize resource use and occupancy. The latter is a perspective of community leaders who work to foster communities and help specific workers.

Historically, the coworking movement emerged from the brotherhood and sisterhood of coworking community leaders who were interested in creating thriving communities and seeking to replicate local and small-scale successes. In addition, the coworking movement offers workers a narrative about creativity, serendipity, and the new way of work.

The social office industry, on the other hand, benefits from these communities while offering efficient and flexible infrastructure. This industry coexists with—but is not really part of—the movement. This industry is driven by the economic imperatives of cost, revenue, and growth, which are tangential to fostering thriving local communities.

8.5. Conclusion

Today the idea of a single, unified coworking movement is somewhat frayed both by explosive growth and by the appropriation of coworking practices and terminology by corporations.

What, then, is the coworking movement? Who does the movement represent? Is the coworking movement part of the service office industry that offers consumer coworking? Or is it a movement of independent workers who form their own authentic communities?

The contemporary concept of coworking has been associated with a movement nearly from its inception. The idea of the coworking movement was articulated in the *Coworking Manifesto* [62], which describes the "new way of work." The movement defines a common identity for the diverse workplaces and workers of the gig economy.

The coworking movement includes workers, community leaders, and operators of work places, who share the goal of fostering thriving communities of workers. However, the movement is important in different ways to different people.

For workers, the coworking movement is a flag of group identity and a guide to the role of coworker. The former is important for socially isolated independent workers. The latter helps workers learn how to be a coworker as well as to articulate the benefits of working to themselves, their peers, and the wider world.

For community leaders, the movement is a guide to the practice of community management. The coworking movement has always been an important connection between the many community leaders.

For workspace operators, the coworking movement is an innovation in social infrastructure, which is a new way to recruit and retain highly mobile digital workers. To successfully fill seats with independent workers, the facility needs both physical infrastructure and social infrastructure—that is, a community of peers. The coworking movement is the core of the social infrastructure.

Chapter References

1. Anderson, Chris. 2012. *Makers*. New York: Random House.
2. Bacigalupo, Tony. 2016. "Consumer Coworking." Global Coworking Unconverence, Los Angeles, May 6. http://canada.gcuc.co/wp-content/uploads/2016/presentations/Consumer%20Coworking%20-%20Tony%20Bacigalupo.pdf
3. Berkun, Scott. 2013. *The Year Without Pants: Wordpress.com and the Future of Work*. San Francisco: Jossey-Bass.
4. Chase, Robin. 2015. *Peers, Inc.: How People and Platforms Are Inventing the Collaborative Economy and Reinventing Capitalism*. New York: PublicAffairs.
5. Chicago Deskpass. 2016. "Chicago Deskpass", accessed January, 2018. https://www.deskpass.com/
6. Citizen Space. 2016. "Citizen Space - A Nicer Place to work", accessed July, 2017. http://citizenspace.us/
7. Coboat. 2017. "Coboat", accessed January, 2018. www.coboat.org/
8. CoPass. 2016. "CoPass", accessed January, 2018. https://copass.org/network
9. Cottle, Frank. 2016. "A Foundation for Change: A single global voicex." Global Coworking Unconference Conference, Los Angeles, May 6. http://canada.gcuc.co/wp-content/uploads/2016/presentations/Foundation%20and%20Giving%20-%20Frank%20Cottle.pdf
10. Cowork Pass. 2016. "Cowork Pass", accessed January, 2016. http://coworkunite.com/cowork-pass/
11. Coworking Africa. 2015. "Coworking Africa conference 2015", accessed January, 2018. http://coworkingafrica.com/
12. Coworking Community Blog. 2011. *Coworking Community Blog*. https://coworking.wordpress.com/
13. Coworking Discussion List. 2016. "Coworking Discussion List", accessed January, 2018. https://groups.google.com/forum/#!forum/coworking
14. Coworking Europe. 2017. *Coworking Europe Blog*. http://coworkingeurope.net/blog/
15. Coworking Europe. 2018. "Coworking Europe Conference", accessed January 2018. http://coworkingeurope.net/
16. coworking.org. 2012. "Coworking Manifesto: The Future of Work", accessed January, 2018. http://coworkingmanifesto.com/
17. De Koven, Bernard. 2013. "The Coworking Connection." *Deep Fun with Bernard De Koven*, August 5. http://www.deepfun.com/the-coworking-connection/

18. Deskmag. 2015. "The History of Coworking", accessed January, 2018. http://www.tiki-toki.com/timeline/entry/156192/The-History-Of-Coworking-Presented-By-Deskmag/#vars!date=1997-05-04_03:19:52!

19. Deskmag. 2016. "about us." http://www.deskmag.com/en/about-us

20. Doctorow, Cory. 2009. *Makers*. New York: Tor.

21. Ebeling, Mick. 2015. *Not Impossible: The Art and Joy of Doing What Couldn't Be Done*. New York: Atria Books.

22. Florida, Richard. 2002. *The Rise of the Creative Class. And How It's Transforming Work, Leisure and Everyday Life*. New York: Basic Books.

23. Freelancers Union. 2018. "The Freelancers Union", accessed January 2018. https://www.freelancersunion.org/

24. Gangplank Collective. 2016. "Manifesto - Gangplank", accessed January, 2018. http://gangplankhq.com/vision/manifesto/

25. Gershenfeld, Neil. 2005. *Fab: The Coming Revolution On Your Desktop-From Personal Computing to Personal Fabrication*. New York: Basic Books.

26. Global Coworking Unconference Conferences (GCUC) 2018. "Global Coworking Unconference Conferences (GCUC) ", accessed January, 2018. http://gcuc.co/

27. Hillman, Alex. 2011. "Coworking Core Values 1 of 5: Sustainability", accessed January, 2018. http://dangerouslyawesome.com/2011/08/coworking-core-values-1-of-5-sustainability/

28. Hillman, Alex. 2011. "Coworking Core Values 2 of 5: Accessibility", accessed January, 2018. http://dangerouslyawesome.com/2011/08/coworking-core-values-2-of-5-accessibility/

29. Hillman, Alex. 2011. "Coworking Core Values 3 of 5: Openness", accessed January, 2018. http://dangerouslyawesome.com/2011/08/coworking-core-values-3-of-5-openness/

30. Hillman, Alex. 2011. "Coworking Core Values 4 of 5: Community", accessed January, 2018. http://dangerouslyawesome.com/2011/08/coworking-core-values-4-of-5-community/

31. Hillman, Alex. 2011. "Coworking Core Values 5 of 5: Collaboration", accessed January, 2018. http://dangerouslyawesome.com/2011/10/coworking-core-values-5-of-5-collaboration/

32. Hillman, Alex. 2016. The problem with the coworking industry in 2016. *New Worker Magazine*. Accessed January, 2018. http://newworker.co/mag/the-problem-with-the-coworking-industry-in-2016/

33. Horowitz, Sara. 2012. *The Freelancer's Bible*. New York: Workman Publishing.

34. Impact Hub. 2016. "Impact Hub - Experience Collaborartion", accessed January, 2018. https://www.impacthub.net/

35. Jacobs, Esther, and André Gussekloo. 2016. *Digital Nomads: How to Live, Work and Play Around the World*. Amazon.com: Self Published.

36. Jeffery, Al. 2016. Three Ways to Co-Create a Vibrant Co-living Culture. *Shareable*. Accessed January, 2018. http://www.shareable.net/blog/three-ways-to-co-create-a-vibrant-co-living-culture

37. Johnson, Cat. 2015. 7 Essential Coworking Resources for Digital Nomads. *Shareable*. Accessed January, 2018. http://www.shareable.net/blog/7-essential-coworking-resources-for-digital-nomads

38. Johnson, Cat. 2016. Look Out, Coworking. Here Comes Big Money. *Shareable*. Accessed January, 2018. http://www.shareable.net/blog/look-out-coworking-here-comes-big-money

39. Johnson, Cat. 2016. Recap of the #FutureOfCoworking Twitter Chat. *Shareable*. Accessed January, 2018. http://www.shareable.net/blog/recap-of-the-futureofcoworking-twitter-chat

40. Kennedy, Pagan. 2016. *Inventology: How We Dream Up Things That Change The World*. Boston: Houghton Miffin Harcourt.

41. Kwiatkowski, Angel. 2011. "Coworking: An Easy Way To Green Your Business." *Cohere Community Blog*, May 9. http://coherecommunity.com/blog/coworking-green-your-business

42. Kwiatkowski, Angel. 2011. "Why Being Social Is More Important Than Social Media." *Cohere Community Blog*, February 23. http://coherecommunity.com/blog/being-social-is-more-important-than-social-media

43. Liquid Talent. 2015. "Dude, Where's My Drone: The future of work and what you can do to prepare for it." https://www.dropbox.com/s/405kr9keucv97gw/LiquidTalentFoWEbook.pdf?dl=0 (accessed January, 2018).

44. Marshall, Claire. 2015. "How to Make Money (and a whole lot more) by Sharing." Self Published. https://www.sharestories.net/the-book (accessed January, 2018).

45. McGrath, Robert. 2014. "You Shall Not Crucify The Internet On This Cross of Bitcoin." *Very Much Wow*, July, 34-37 http://issuu.com/verymuchwow/docs/vmw3/35?e=11558635/8421855.

46. McLaren, Diana. 2015. Australian Coworking Event a Window into Growing Movement. *Shareable*. Accessed January, 2018. http://www.shareable.net/blog/australian-coworking-event-a-window-into-growing-movement

47. Mesku, Melissa. 2016. Community: the key thing. *New Worker Magazine*. Accessed January, 2018. http://newworker.co/mag/what-your-key-says-about-your-coworking-space/

48. Mok, Kimberley. 2016. "Can co-working vacations offer a better work-life balance?" *Treehuggger*, September 22. http://www.treehugger.com/culture/coworkations-better-work-life-balance.html

49. Neuberg, Brad. 2014. "The Start of Coworking (from the Guy that Started It)." *coding in paradise*, January 16. http://codinginparadise.org/ebooks/html/blog/start_of_coworking.html

50. New Worker Magazine. 2016. About. Accessed January, 2018. http://newworker.co/mag/about/

51. NextSpace. 2016. "NextSpace", accessed January, 2016. http://nextspace.us/

52. Nomad House. 2018. "Nomad House - Start your online business while exploring some of the most beautiful places", accessed January, 2018. https://nomadhouse.io/

53. Olma, Sebastian. 2012. "The Serendipity Machine: A Disruptive Business Model for Society 3.0." https://www.seats2meet.com/downloads/The_Serendipity_Machine.pdf (accessed January 2018).

54. Open Coworking. 2016. "Open Coworking - Building the movement together", accessed January, 2018. http://opencoworking.org/

55. Popper, Nathaniel. 2015. *Digital Gold: Bitcoin And The Inside Story of The Misfits and Millionaires Trying to Reinvent Money*. New York: HarperCollins.

56. Scholz, Trebor. 2016. Platform Cooperativism: Challenging the Corporate Sharing Economy. New York: Rosa Luxemburg Stiftung: New York Office http://www.rosalux-nyc.org/platform-cooperativism-2/.

57. Seattle Collaborative Space Alliance. 2016. "Seattle Collaborative Space Alliance (SCSA)", accessed January, 2018. http://collaborativespaces.org/

58. Stark, Kevin. 2017. Oxford Internet Institute Launches Interactive Map of the Global Gig Economy. *Shareable*. Accessed January, 2018. http://www.shareable.net/blog/oxford-internet-institute-launches-interactive-map-of-the-global-gig-economy

59. Sundesk. 2016. "Sundesk: Coworking in Taghazout, Morocco", accessed January, 2016. http://www.sun-desk.com/

60. The CoWorking Institute. 2015. "The CoWorking Institute", accessed January, 2016. http://coworking.net/

61. The Coworking Pass Europe. 2016. "The Coworking Pass Europe", accessed January, 2016. http://www.lespotmultiburo.com/coworking-pass-en/

62. The Coworking Wiki. 2015. "Coworking Manifesto (global - for the world) " *The Coworking Wiki*. http://wiki.coworking.org/w/page/35382594/Coworking%20Manifesto%20%28global%20-%20for%20the%20world%29

63. The Coworking Wiki. 2015. "The Values of Open Coworking", accessed January, 2018. http://wiki.coworking.org/w/page/67817489/The%20Values%20of%20Open%20Coworking

64. The Coworking Wiki. 2016. "The Coworking Wiki", accessed January, 2018. http://wiki.coworking.org/w/page/16583831/FrontPage

65. The Global Coworking Blog. 2015. *The Global Coworking Blog*. http://blog.coworking.com/

66. The League of Extraordinary Coworking Spaces. 2016. "The League of Extraordinary Coworking Spaces", accessed January, 2018. http://lexc.org/

67. The Surf Office. 2015. "The Surf Office Santa Cruz", accessed January, 2018. http://www.thesurfoffice.com/santa-cruz/

68. WeWork. 2015. "WeWork: Create Your Life's Work", accessed January, 2018. https://www.wework.com/

69. Widdicombe, Lizzie. 2016. "Happy together." *The New Yorker*, May 16, 48-55.

70. Wikipedia. 2016. "Open-source model", accessed January, 2018. https://en.wikipedia.org/wiki/Open-source_model

Part V. Conclusion: What Is Coworking?

Chapter 9: What Is Coworking, and What Do We Know about Coworking?

"What is coworking?"

From earlier chapters, it should be clear that coworking is a diverse phenomenon, so there is no simple and definitive answer to this question. Even if a precise definition of coworking is elusive, there is a lot that can be said about coworking spaces, contemporary workers, and communities.

Section 9.1 pulls together the key features that seem to define the essence of contemporary coworking: a face-to-face community of independent workers.

Section 9.2 summarizes the most important points from earlier chapters.

9.1. What Is Coworking?

Coworking is part of a varied landscape of contemporary work places and practices, and it can be difficult to draw a firm boundary around the term and the practice.

It is difficult to delineate a specific type of work that is coworking or particular workers who are coworkers. Independent workers perform the same activities at home, in a public café, or at a rented desk in a coworking space. For that matter, many independent workers use several workplaces from day to day, possibly including more than one coworking space.

It is also difficult to identify a specific type of workplace that is a coworking space. There are many kinds of spaces that have infrastructure that is similar to a coworking space. Coworking spaces are operated in rental office complexes and business incubators but also in libraries, resorts, and private homes. Also, there may be a very fine line between a coffee shop—or other public space where workers congregate—and a dedicated coworking space.

It is also true that one of the outstanding features of contemporary coworking is the tremendous diversity of coworking spaces and coworkers. Beyond basic infrastructure, many different physical designs and organizational principles have been tried. More important, the overall population of coworkers and coworking spaces is a diverse collection of local communities. Each coworking space is inhabited by a community of workers with its own workplace culture.

Nevertheless, there are some critical features that generally distinguish coworking from other similar workspaces and work practices.

Bob's Definition of Coworking

Coworking is a work place that is used by independent workers, generally with flexible, on-demand rental agreements. Notably, the workers do not work for the owner/operator of the workspace and the workers, not their employers, select their workplace. A coworking space is a place where a group of independent workers have physical, face-to-face social interactions, which is generally called a community. In this sense, a coworking space is a real-world physical realization of a digital social network.

Any workplace with these characteristics is clearly a coworking space, whether it is called that or not. Other spaces might be called a coworking space, but if they lack one or more of these features, they really aren't.

9.2. What Do We Know about Coworking?

However coworking may be defined, there are quite a few things that can be said about coworking and coworking spaces. It seems that coworking "works," at least for some workers some of the time. Coworking spaces and their communities are flourishing, and they appear to make workers happy and successful.

This section summarizes the key findings discussed in earlier chapters.

Coworking Is Driven by and Enables the Gig Economy

First, coworking is both created by the gig economy and is a response to the contingencies of this new way of work. In the freelance economy, independent workers are generally responsible for providing their own digital infrastructure and working environment. Coworking spaces and communities were created by these workers to meet these needs. A coworking space is designed to be where gig workers work.

Contemporary independent workers often work on demand and require resources, including digital infrastructure, office space, and collaborators, as needed. Ubiquitous digital technology enables remote working and remote collaboration from anywhere on the planet.

But digital interaction is not sufficient workers need *social infrastructure* in the form of other workers. The presence of peers is a source of mutual help and professional collaboration. In addition, colleagues offer conviviality and relief from the isolation of independent work.

In short, a coworking space is ideally designed for gig workers. Freelance workers benefit from a coworking space that enables their work and from the support of a community of peers. When it works well, a coworking space is one of the most effective places where the work of the gig economy happens.

Coworking (Probably) Makes (Some) Workers Happy

For workers, the first, and most important fact about coworking is that *coworking makes workers happy*. Empirical evidence suggests that coworkers like coworking and that they "thrive" in coworking spaces. As the veteran researchers from Michigan comment, this level of "thriving" is "unheard of" in the literature of work places [10].

These studies also suggest that coworking has other benefits as well. Coworkers frequently report greater productivity, collaborative networking, and "serendipity"—at least compared to working alone. Many of these benefits stem from social interactions and with the community of coworkers who inhabit the coworking space.

As discussed in chapter 7, these findings should be taken with caution. The data is weak, mainly self-reported, and probably not representative of all workers and workplaces. It is probably most accurate to say that coworking makes *some* workers happy, at least for a time.

Perhaps the key feature of coworking is that, unlike conventional workplaces, workers are allowed to choose their own work environment. The on-demand design of coworking means that workers *choose* to work in a particular coworking space and with a particular group of coworkers. They work only in ways they wish and so long as they wish. Everything else equal, self-selection should assure that coworkers are happy with their current workspace.

However, even if coworking isn't as beneficial as the studies suggest, making workers happy—even just some workers for some time—is not a small thing! Making workers happy may or may not make them more productive, but making workers *unhappy* certainly does not make them more productive.

Coworking Is All about Community

To reiterate one of the main themes of the book, a coworking space is a space inhabited by a community of workers. In some ways, coworking is a "materialization" of a digital community. A coworking space offers the virtues of a digital community (professional networking, knowledge sharing, creative collaboration, etc.), with the conviviality of interacting with real people, face to face.

These face-to-face interactions are one of the key factors that make coworkers happy. As Zachary Klaas puts it, for the contemporary digitally connected but socially disconnected, a coworking space is a "respite from our isolation" [6]. Workers find beneficial opportunities for collaboration, networking, and creative "serendipity" [9, 8, 7, 1, 10]. But most of all, a coworking community is an opportunity for altruism, mutual help, and sharing—behaviors that make people happy. As Lori Kane describes her home coworking space, it is "a friendship incubator" [4, 5, 3].

For many workers, membership in a coworking community offers a sense of communal identity, both as part of a group of "people like me" and as part of a world-wide new way of working. At the same time, a strong face-to-face community that provides personal identity to its members may also become insular, "tribal," or exclusionary. No community can satisfy all workers.

However, there are a great variety of successful coworking communities, and most workers have a choice of several local coworking spaces. This diversity is an important key to the success of coworking. Workers select a coworking space ad community that meets their current needs and preferences. It is very likely that self-selecting one's own working environment and colleagues makes workers happy.

Coworking Can Be Thought of as Participatory Theater

Chapter 7 presented the idea that coworking can be considered participatory theater. Workers are invited to enact the role of coworker as part of an epic story about their own life and work.

Chapter 9: What Do We Know About Coworking?

The script is a loose narrative set forth by coworking leaders, fellow workers, and documents such as the *Coworking Manifesto* [11]. The classic coworking play might be described something like,

> A group of scrappy (young) freelancers, banding together to help each other succeed and have fun along the way.

The idea of "coworking as participatory theater" gives interesting insights into coworking, coworking communities, leadership, and the space itself.

When a worker joins a coworking community, he or she implicitly signs up to learn the role of "successful, happy coworker." Playing out his part, the worker *acts as*, and thereby *becomes*, a successful and happy worker. Participating in this story also gives her work additional meaning. She isn't just showing up and completing her own assignments; she is also supporting and collaborating with her peers, and together they are pioneering the new economy and making the world better.

The coworking narrative is not a one-person show. Workers are part of an ensemble cast in a story about supporting and collaborating with their peers. As in an improvised theatrical performance, workers must attend to their fellows, react to developments, and hold up their end of dialogs. This process itself can be both challenging and rewarding.

Community leaders have a role similar to the facilitator of an improvised play. They explain the scenario, introduce and instruct the players, and set up scenes, such as communal events. In this sense, Alex Hillman's call for coworking leaders to act like *tummlers* is particularly apt [2].

From this perspective, the coworking space itself is *a theater set* in which the improvised performance occurs. Like the set for a play, the design of the space may influence the action but does not tell the story. In theater, a story can be performed on many different sets, and different stories can be done in the same setting. Similarly, there is no one "right" space for coworking, and many different physical spaces are used for coworking.

However, just as a play needs to be performed *somewhere*, coworking requires a physical space. In particular, meeting and talking to peers in person, face to face, is *the* big deal about coworking. An adequate physical space is critical for the whole enterprise.

9.3. Conclusion

Coworking is difficult to define for several reasons. Coworking is hard to clearly distinguish from many other similar work environments. Second, workers' status as a coworker is difficult to define because his or her commitment to that status is neither exclusive nor continuous and may be very informal. And third, coworking spaces and coworkers are extremely diverse, encompassing a great variety of physical spaces and work cultures.

In the face of this uncertainty, one feature that seems to define and distinguish coworking is that a coworking space is inhabited by a self-selected community of independent workers. Evidence suggests that coworking makes workers happy and may improve productivity, creativity, and serendipity. Whether every worker will accrue these benefits or not, it seems clear that coworking succeeds mostly because workers find a face-to-face community in the coworking space.

Two other features of contemporary coworking stand out.

First, coworking communities are served by skilled leaders who create and sustain the culture of the workplace. Leaders play a crucial role in inducting workers, sustaining social relations, and defining the culture of the group. This role has become formalized to become a new profession.

Second, a local coworking community is participatory culture, which workers enact. Participating in the community gives these independent workers social status and personal identity as part of the group and possibly as part of a movement. This identity gives their life and work additional significance.

Chapter References

1. Bacigalupo, Tony. 2015. "No More Sink Full of Mugs." New York: No More Sink Full of Mugs. https://sellfy.com/p/IBtB/ (accessed January, 2018).
2. Hillman, Alex. 2014. "To build a strong community, stop "community managing", be a Tummler instead." *Alex Hillman*, April 20. http://dangerouslyawesome.com/2014/04/community-management-tummling-a-tale-of-two-mindsets/
3. Johnson, Cat. 2015. The Top 10 Tips For Running a Coworking Space at Home. *Shareable*. Accessed January, 2018. http://www.shareable.net/blog/the-top-10-tips-for-running-a-coworking-space-at-home
4. Kane, Lori. 2012. "What is a friendship incubator?", accessed April, 2016. http://www.collectiveself.com/frequently-asked-questions/what-is-a-friendship-incubator/
5. Kane, Lori, Tabitha Borchardt, and Bas de Baar. 2015. *Reimagination Stations: Creating a Game-Changing In-Home Coworking Space*: Lori Kane.
6. Klaas, Zachary R. 2014. Coworking & Connectivity in Berlin. University of Illinois at Urbana Champaign https://www.academia.edu/11486279/Coworking_Connectivity.
7. Kwiatkowski, Angel, and Beth Buczynski. 2011. "Coworking: Building Community as a Space Catalyst." Ft. Collins: Cohere Coworking. http://coherecommunity.com/shop/coworking-building-community-as-a-space-catalyst (accessed January, 2018).
8. Liquid Talent. 2015. "Dude, Where's My Drone: The future of work and what you can do to prepare for it." https://www.dropbox.com/s/405kr9keucv97gw/LiquidTalentFoWEbook.pdf?dl=0 (accessed January, 2018).
9. Olma, Sebastian. 2012. "The Serendipity Machine: A Disruptive Business Model for Society 3.0." https://www.seats2meet.com/downloads/The_Serendipity_Machine.pdf (accessed January 2018).
10. Spreitzer, Gretchen, Peter Bacevice, and Lyndon Garrett. 2015. "Why People Thrive in Coworking Spaces." *Harvard Business Review* 93 (8):1-7. https://hbr.org/2015/05/why-people-thrive-in-coworking-spaces
11. The Coworking Wiki. 2015. "Coworking Manifesto (global - for the world) " *The Coworking Wiki*. http://wiki.coworking.org/w/page/35382594/Coworking%20Manifesto%20%28global%20-%20for%20the%20world%29

Chapter 10: The Future of Coworking

This final chapter turns to the future of coworking.

What is the future of coworking? What is the future of coworkers?

Coworking as we know it is a recent innovation, closely associated with the Internet and the gig economy that have developed in the early twenty-first century. The number of freelance workers has grown rapidly, as has the number of independent contractors and small companies, and these workers are attracted to coworking spaces. The number of coworking spaces and coworkers has grown rapidly in the last decade even as many coworking spaces have closed in the same period.

These successes have led to optimistic projections that coworking will be a key part of a new economy and a new way of work [12, 15]. Is coworking indeed the future of workplaces?

This chapter briefly looks at three related questions about the future of coworking.

1. Is coworking sustainable?
2. Is coworking scalable?
3. How diverse will coworking become?

The conclusion sums up with a brief vision of what coworking may look like in the future.

10.1. Is Coworking Sustainable?

Is coworking sustainable over time? Will coworking spaces and communities continue to exist for significant periods of time? Will workers cowork over the course of their entire career?

Coworking Churn

For the last decade, there has been a very large amount of "churn" in both coworking spaces and the workers inhabiting them. New coworking spaces open every week while existing spaces close, and large numbers of workers join and leave individual coworking spaces each year. Sustaining a coworking space and community requires constantly recruiting new workers and retaining as many current members as possible.

This churn is inherent in the nature of contemporary coworking. Coworking is a temporary and contingent relationship between individual workers and the workplace. An individual worker may occupy a seat for as little as a few hours at a time, and he or she may choose when and for how long they use the space. Notably, workers have no formal allegiance to either the workplace or the other workers there.

This loose association means that an individual worker can join a coworking community for a while and then move to another workplace. Indeed, from day to day, an independent worker might work at home, in a conventional office, and at a coworking space, or even alternate among several coworking spaces in a single workday. Workers generally remain in a specific coworking community for no more than a year or two. The upshot is that the population of coworkers is constantly changing, and membership in any specific coworking community is fluid.

Coworking spaces generally operate at the edge of economic viability. Changes in membership or costs have forced many spaces to close. It isn't surprising, then, that most coworking spaces have been open only a few years, and many close after only a few years of operation. Thus, in most places, there has been a fluid population of workspaces as well as workers.

Still, despite high turnover of both workers and workspaces, coworking has continued to grow rapidly. The growth represents a large number of new workers, new coworking operations, and expansions of existing operations.

Such rapid growth in the face of heavy churn raises fundamental questions about sustainability. As long as the population of both workplaces and workers is extremely dynamic, it can change very rapidly. In a particular city or area, coworking could easily fall as fast as it has risen. Indeed, the very nature of coworking could quickly alter, along with the communities of workers.

In short, the rapid churn means that it is extremely difficult to project the future of coworking.

Sustaining a Community

How well will local coworking communities persist?

"Sustaining a community" is partly a matter of definition. What is the community in question? Is it a specific set of people? Or is it whatever group inhabits a particular workplace? For that matter, who is a member? What must a worker do in order to be part of the community?

It is difficult to define exactly who belongs to a coworking community. In many ways, a coworking community is like "my grandfather's axe" [19]: the community has an individual identity, but it gradually or rapidly morphs as individual workers join and leave. As a coworking space operates over several years, the community and its local culture will surely evolve as the roster of workers changes.

Belonging to a coworking community isn't just a matter of paying rent; it requires interaction with other workers, participating in events, and so on. Furthermore, membership in a community is a social and psychological status: workers identify themselves with and are recognized as part of a particular group of like-minded individuals.

Coworking spaces haven't existed for very long, so there isn't really much information about the evolution of coworking communities. It appears that some communities are fragile, disappearing in a short time. Others persist, sometimes even after the coworking space itself has closed. Still others might continue to exist but transform into a quite different group culture.

One factor that is crucial to a thriving, long-lasting community is leadership, which sustains and shapes the coworking community as it evolves. A change or loss of key leaders might well lead to the dissolution of a coworking community, even if the workspace remains open.

In short, the future success of coworking depends on sustaining communities of workers, but it isn't easy to predict the future of coworking communities in general or of any given community.

Coworking for a Whole Career?

Is coworking something that workers will continue to do over their whole working life?

The short-term and low-cost commitment of coworking is well suited to part-time or marginal employment and to the early phases of starting a business. It is also suited to a rootless, digital nomadism. But will workers thrive and be satisfied for longer term?

One perspective on these questions comes from several surveys that all suggest three common reasons why coworkers leave their current workplace (e.g., [4]):

- Relocation to a new city
- Inability to pay membership
- Due to full-time employment or business expansion

Together, these findings suggest that workers stop coworking when they are either *successful* or when they are *unsuccessful*. It seems that even if a worker thrives in a coworking space, his or her career may well outgrow the coworking space. In short, a worker's business needs may change over his or her career.

A worker may choose full-time employment with a workplace and colleagues. In general, a successful long-term collaboration or conventional employment will require a permanent, dedicated workplace. Similarly, a successful business will want its own space. For a growing business, it is important to have an identifiable, dedicated space for customer relations and branding.

Workers' personal needs and preferences also may change over time. While any worker may benefit from and enjoy the synergy of a coworking community, the facilities and group culture of a coworking space simply may not be psychologically compatible as a worker ages. A middle-aged worker or young parent may find that a community of single twenty-something fresh-outs may no longer feel like a group of "like-minded peers."

Many coworking spaces lack features important for working parents or older workers, such as access to childcare, parking, or physical accessibility. In addition, the features a coworking space does offer may have less appeal for older workers. For example, twenty-four-hour access and common amenities such as video games, film nights, and cocktail party mixers may not be as attractive to married parents with young children as they are to younger, single workers.

In addition, a mature worker may well not benefit as much from a coworking community. A worker with an established career will have a social network of peers and colleagues, an established reputation, and an identity as a successful entrepreneur or worker. And, as workers become immersed in the social responsibilities of marriage, childrearing, and elder care, they will have less time and inclination to participate in a workplace community of any kind.

In short, for many workers, coworking might be suitable for a rather short period in their careers, perhaps when they are just starting out or are temporarily underemployed.

What Would "Life-Long" Coworking Look Like?

While workers and their businesses may outgrow their first coworking space and community, coworking certainly *could* evolve to attract older and more established workers.

Coworking spaces might be integrated into other aspects of living, including housing and childrearing. For example, coworking may be collocated with childcare, elementary schools, and grocery stores. Going even farther, some workers may prefer arrangements resembling "coliving" or "cohousing," which also incorporate shared workspace. This approach might combine shared living (e.g., [13, 18]) and aging in place (e.g., [7, 10]) with home coworking (e.g., [11, 9]) in a multigenerational living and working community.

In addition, the events and community interactions could be geared for a range of ages and including family members. Parents of small children are not interested in singles mixers but might enjoy kids' activities.

In short, coworking spaces can serve workers throughout their career, but facilities and services will have to evolve far beyond today's operations.

10.2. Is Coworking Scalable?

However it is defined, coworking has grown extremely rapidly over the past decade from almost nothing to tens of thousands of workspaces and a million or so workers. Nevertheless, coworking still represents a small fraction of the total workforce, and it remains to be seen if this growth will continue.

Coworking overall scales along two main dimensions: the number of workers (members) and the number of individual coworking spaces (or coworking communities). A third, related dimension is the size of an individual coworking space (community).

Number of Workers

Will the number of workers choosing to cowork continue to increase?

The future of coworking depends on the future of workers and working. How will workers wish to work or be constrained to work? Which workers will use coworking spaces? What sorts of work will be done in coworking spaces?

One of the forces driving the growth of coworking has been the worldwide growth of the gig economy, which has created hundreds of thousands of freelance workers, independent contractors, and remote workers. Will the gig economy continue to grow, and if so, will this drive further growth in coworking?

The current size of the gig economy is difficult to determine. In part, this is due to imprecise definitions of what should be counted. Some estimates include almost all part-time workers, including hobbyists, moonlighters, and pensioners (e.g., [5, 6]). Others include many kinds of digitally enabled pieceworkers (e.g., Uber or UpWork) and even people who monetize assets (e.g., AirBnB). The picture is even murkier because a person may have several sources of income, which shift over time. Finally, there is little solid data to track these activities [16].

Only a small fraction of all independent workers are likely to choose and be able to pay for coworking, so it is important to understand the composition of this workforce. To project the number of coworkers in the future, the total size of the gig economy is less important than the number and types of high-paid independent workers.

It seems likely that the number of digital workers will continue to grow and that many of them will work as independent freelancers. Other digital workers will choose to work remotely—that is, as a long-term employee but not in a conventional office. Whether coworking will expand beyond the digital industries remains to be seen.

Individual entrepreneurs and small startups may choose coworking spaces, perhaps being part of a business incubator. These entrepreneurs may be classified as contractors or self-employed workers, but in any case, a successful startup will grow rapidly, hire workers, and so will outgrow coworking.

It is likely that growing numbers of professionals, such as consultants, lawyers, and accountants, may choose coworking, at least part of the time. However, these occupations generally need appropriate branded space, securing intellectual property, and privacy for their clients.

Finally, there is a large range of workers who may or may not choose coworking in the future. These might include

- People who work requires physical tools, shop or studio space, fabrication or assembly processes
- People who work with human clients, like teachers and therapists
- Retail businesses that require branded space and foot traffic

The coworking model could incorporate facilities for these activities, though not every workspace will have every feature.

The Size of Coworking Communities

Assuming that the number of potential coworkers continues to grow, will the number of coworking spaces also grow? Or will individual coworking spaces become larger? How large can or should a single coworking space and community grow?

Any given coworking space needs to attract and retain sufficient members to cover costs. However, there are many choices and variations of costs and revenue sources, so there is no simple or universal formula for the minimum number workers needed to sustain a given workspace.

In the past few years, coworking spaces have ranged in size from a handful of seats up to many hundreds. Some operations have multiple sites, with aggregate memberships in the thousands or tens of thousands. Clearly, there are potential economies of scale in a larger space, as well as opportunity for higher and steadier revenues.

A larger group of workers also provides a larger social network and pool of potential collaborators. This should increase business opportunities and synergy for the workers. However, it is far from clear whether a larger population of workers enhances or detracts from a community spirit and the concomitant benefits of working in a shared space.

Growing a coworking community will change it, possibly beyond recognition. Research indicates that social networks generally are not larger than 100 to 200 people (e.g. [3, 2, 14]) and that larger groups tend to break into subgroups or hierarchical networks [1]. A workspace may host a dozen workers or a thousand, but it seems likely that there will be different kinds of communities depending on the size of the group.

The Number of Coworking Spaces (Communities)

Coworkers are usually attracted to the community of workers in a space more than the physical space itself. This means that the number of coworking spaces in an area is determined by the number of communities.

There are many factors that play into the success of a coworking community besides the number of workers. The culture and psychology of the community may set expectations for participation and social interactions that favor a small or larger community.

10.3. A More Diverse Future

The number of coworkers may well continue to grow, but scaling up a coworking community is not as simple as acquiring larger space. Growth will bring in a more diverse population of workers. Some coworking spaces will grow much larger, but it is likely that there will be a diverse selection of workspaces of different sizes.

If coworking does grow to include a much larger and diverse set of workers, the diversity will be reflected not only in the demographics of the workers, but also in the design of the workspaces and the culture of coworking communities. Creating new coworking communities will require conscious attention to the needs and preferences of workers, particularly workers who do not choose today's coworking spaces. Coworking leaders will have an outsized impact on this growth because leaders represent and articulate the values of their community.

How Diverse Are Coworking Communities Today?

It is frequently observed that coworking spaces attract workers similar to the digital industry: heavily young, single, pale, and male (e.g., [11]). However, the picture is not so simple.

Each coworking space is a relatively small, local community of likeminded workers. Such a community is bound to be homogenous because the workers in any one workspace generally share interests, attitudes, and occupations. This sameness may be by design (e.g., based on notions of how freelancers succeed [15]), circumstantial (e.g., due to the demographics of the city [17]), or strategic (e.g., to differentiate the workspace [8]).

In any given area, there will likely be a number of coworking spaces, and each may reflect its local neighborhood, certain types of work, or a distinct vibe. In a large city, workers can choose which workplace and community they wish to join. The upshot is that the total population of coworkers is more heterogeneous that any individual community.

The Future of Coworking Will Be Even More Diverse

Following this line of reasoning, as coworking grows and serves workers who are not currently coworking, it will become more diverse. This will play out several ways.

Some coworking operations will grow larger, with more workers per location and more locations. The workers in these sites will probably be more heterogeneous than today, if only because they will represent a larger slice of the whole population. Furthermore, the dynamics of communities and social networks predict that a larger group will naturally fissure into multiple networks or communities sharing the same workspace.

There will also be new coworking spaces designed to serve new or underserved groups of workers. These operations will seek to distinguish themselves with facilities and a vibe that attracts their target workers. For example, a space might aim to serve a specific location (e.g., a city neighborhood or a rural area). Or a coworking operation might target specific types of work or occupation, such as law, accounting, or other professional services.

A coworking space might recruit workers with specific demographics, such as professional women, married parents, or older workers. This strategy would be reflected in many aspects of the design and culture of the coworking space. The décor, soundscape, entertainment facilities, and general culture will adapt to the needs and preferences of different workers.

In the future, coworking may well integrate with a variety of other facets of life. For example, some coworking spaces will have onsite childcare (or alternatively, some childcare providers will offer onsite coworking). For that matter, a variety of coliving spaces may develop, incorporating living and work spaces.

In short, the landscape of coworking will be a patchwork of different-sized workspaces serving different communities with different vibes.

10.4. Conclusion

Coworking is likely to persist and grow in the future, though the workers, workspaces, and workplace cultures will be even more diverse than they are today. The future of coworking probably will look a lot like the dining and hospitality industries today.

This analogy is actually quite deep. Working, like eating, is a physical and embodied activity. There can be no purely virtual workplace any more than there can be a purely virtual dining room. In fact, coworking spaces came to exist in the first place to provide a physical location for virtual work and virtual organizations.

Everyone needs to eat and work. But one person only eats (works) some of the time and in only one place at a time. Furthermore, an individual may choose a different eatery (workplace) each day, and his preferences may well change over time.

Thus, coworking can be sustained in the same ways that local food services thrive. A city or region may support a variety of coworking spaces, patronized by the evolving population of independent workers. Some workspaces will provide a consistent, standardized "commodity" service, and others might offer their own unique, "authentic" local experience, Workers may well use several workspaces for different purposes. Over his or her career, a worker will choose workplaces according to his or her changing needs and preferences.

As in the case of restaurants, a coworking space attracts and retains workers by the design and amenities of the space. But a coworking space must also develop a vibe and identity that represents the values of its community. Developing a local culture is a deliberate and conscious design process that cannot be done with an algorithmic cookie cutter.

Just as restaurant service defines the eating experience, coworking community leadership will play a critical role in the success of coworking. A community leader personally represents, articulates, and lives out the values of the community more than any physical layout ever could.

Chapter References

1. Buchanan, Mark. 2002. *Nexus: Small Worlds and the Groundbreaking Theory of Networks*. New York: W. W. Norton and Company.
2. De Solla Price, Derik J., and Donald Beaver. 1966. "Collaboration in an Invisible College." *American Psychologist.* 21 (11):1011-1018
3. Dunbar, R. I. M. 1992. "Neocortex size as a constraint on group size in primates." *Journal of Human Evolution* 22 (6):469-493. doi: 10.1016/0047-2484(92)90081-J. http://www.sciencedirect.com/science/article/pii/004724849290081J
4. Foertsch, Carsten. 2016. 2016 Global Coworking Survey. *Deskmag*. Accessed January, 2018. http://www.deskmag.com/en/2016-forecast-global-coworking-survey-results/2
5. Freelancers Union. 2016. Freelancing in America: 2016. New York: Freelancers Union and Upwork https://fu-prod-storage.s3.amazonaws.com/content/None/FreelancinginAmerica2016report.pdf.
6. Freelancers Union, and UpWork. 2017. Freelancing in America: 2017. Freelancers Union https://s3.amazonaws.com/fuwt-prod-storage/content/FreelancingInAmericaReport-2017.pdf.
7. Glass, Anne P. 2012. Aging Better Together. (2). Accessed January, 2018. http://www.secondjourney.org/itin/12_Sum/12Sum_Glass.htm
8. HeraHub. 2017. "Hera Hub: Workspace for Women", accessed January 2015. http://herahub.com/
9. Hoffice. 2017. "Hoffice: Come and work at someone's home", accessed January, 2018. http://hoffice.nu/en/
10. Johnson, Cat. 2016. Aging in Community: Inside the Senior Cohousing Movement. *Shareable*. http://www.shareable.net/blog/aging-in-community-inside-the-senior-cohousing-movement
11. Kane, Lori, Tabitha Borchardt, and Bas de Baar. 2015. *Reimagination Stations: Creating a Game-Changing In-Home Coworking Space*: Lori Kane.
12. Liquid Talent. 2015. "Dude, Where's My Drone: The future of work and what you can do to prepare for it." https://www.dropbox.com/s/405kr9keucv97gw/LiquidTalentFoWEbook.pdf?dl=0 (accessed January, 2018).
13. Martin, Courtney E. 2016. *The New Better Off: Reinventing the American Dream*. Berkeley: Seal Press.
14. Miritello, Giovanna, Esteban Moro, Rubén Lara, Rocío Martínez-López, Sam G. B. Roberts, and Robin I. M. Dunbar. 2013. Time as a

Limited Resource: Communication Strategy in Mobile Phone Networks. arXiv https://arxiv.org/abs/1301.2464.

15. Olma, Sebastian. 2012. "The Serendipity Machine: A Disruptive Business Model for Society 3.0." https://www.seats2meet.com/downloads/The_Serendipity_Machine. pdf (accessed January 2018).

16. Oxford International Institute. 2016. "Introducing the iLabour Project", accessed January, 2018. http://ilabour.oii.ox.ac.uk/

17. The Harlem Collective. 2017. "The Harlem Collective", accessed January, 2018. http://www.theharlemcollective.co/

18. Thompson, Claire. 2012. Cohousing: The Secret to Sustainable Urban Living? *Grist*. Accessed January, 2018. http://grist.org/cities/cohousing-the-secret-to-sustainable-urban-living/

19. Wikipedia. 2017. "Ship of Theseus", accessed January, 2018. https://en.wikipedia.org/wiki/Ship_of_Theseus

Acknowledgements

This book started in part from participation in a peer review panel for a US National Science Foundation program, Virtual Organizations as Sociotechnical Systems. Thanks also to Professor Sally Jackson and Matt Cho who let me tell them why this is an interesting topic.

Thanks for encouraging remarks from Cat Johnson and others at the Global Coworking Unconference in 2016. And thanks for the generous time from Brian Watson of Proximity Space and Kyle at the Sandbox Santa Barbara.

Where the Internet failed to deliver, I found important research materials at the University of Illinois Library and the Urbana Free Library.

The always inspiring Claire Marshall gave important feedback on the first draft.

Dane Torbek did a great (and rapid) edit. Tyra Seldon of the Tyra Seldon Writing Group guided the final production.

Bibliography

1628. 2017. "1628 | A curated co-working space", accessed January, 2018.
  http://www.1628ltd.com/

[Co][Lab]. 2018. "[Co][Lab] Urbana", accessed January, 2018.
  http://colaburbana.com/

Allen, Tammy D., Timothy D. Golden, and Kristen M. Shockley. 2015.
  "How Effective Is Telecommuting? Assessing the Status of Our
  Scientific Findings." *Psychological Science in the Public Interest*
  16 (2):40-68. doi: 10.1177/1529100615593273.
  http://psi.sagepub.com/content/16/2/40.abstract

Amador, Ceci. 2016. "How Coworking Changes your City." *GCUC
  Blog+Press*, March 29. http://usa.gcuc.co/how-coworking-changes-
  your-city/

Amador, Cecilia. 2016. "Learn About Hospitality from the Operator that Got
  it Right." *AllWork*, April 6. https://allwork.space/2016/04/learn-
  about-hospitality-from-the-operator-that-got-it-right/

Anderson, Chris. 2012. *Makers*. New York: Random House.

Andrus, Aubre. 2015. 7 coworking spaces with childcare designed for better
  work-life balance. *Mashable*.
  http://mashable.com/2015/06/13/coworking-spaces-with-
  childcare/#d7StDjnSyZqm

Andrus, Aubre. 2015. "What it takes to set up a successful coworking space
  with childcare." *Mashable*, July 6.
  http://mashable.com/2015/06/06/coworking-spaces-
  childcare/#qbVyas3Vriqz

Bacigalupo, Tony. 2015. "No More Sink Full of Mugs." New York: No
  More Sink Full of Mugs. https://sellfy.com/p/IBtB/ (accessed
  January, 2018).

Bacigalupo, Tony. 2016. "Consumer Coworking." Global Coworking
  Unconverence, Los Angeles, May 6. http://canada.gcuc.co/wp-
  content/uploads/2016/presentations/Consumer%20Coworking%20-
  %20Tony%20Bacigalupo.pdf

Baug, Kelly. 2014. Having it all: coworking with childcare. *New Worker
  Magazine*. Accessed January, 2018.
  http://newworker.co/mag/working-parents-coworking-with-
  childcare/

Berkun, Scott. 2013. *The Year Without Pants: Wordpress.com and the
  Future of Work*. San Francisco: Jossey-Bass.

Bhagwandin, Stefan. 2016. The sustainability of luxury coworking spaces.
  New Worker Magazine. Accessed January, 2018.

http://newworker.co/mag/the-sustainability-of-luxury-coworking-spaces/

Big Bounce. 2016. "Big Bounce – Keeping Arizona startups in business", accessed January, 2018. http://www.bigbounce.co/

BlogFabrik. 2016. "Blogfabrik - Empowering Content Creators", accessed January, 2018. http://blogfabrik.de/en/

Boushey, Heather, J. Bradford DeLong, and Marshall Steinbaum. 2017. *After Piketty: The Agenda for Economics and Inequality.* Cambridge, MA: Harvard University Press.

Buchanan, Mark. 2002. *Nexus: Small Worlds and the Groundbreaking Theory of Networks*. New York: W. W. Norton and Company.

Buczynski, Beth. 2011. Coworking as a Business: Which Model Is Best? *Sharable*. Accessed January, 2018. http://www.shareable.net/blog/coworking-as-a-business-which-model-is-best

Buczynski, Beth. 2011. What Coworking Brings To The Community Table. *Sharable*. Accessed January, 2018. http://www.shareable.net/blog/what-coworking-brings-to-the-community-table

Chase, Robin. 2015. *Peers, Inc.: How People and Platforms Are Inventing the Collaborative Economy and Reinventing Capitalism*. New York: PublicAffairs.

Chicago Deskpass. 2016. "Chicago Deskpass", accessed January, 2018. https://www.deskpass.com/

Citizen Space. 2016. "Citizen Space - A Nicer Place to work", accessed July, 2017. http://citizenspace.us/

Coboat. 2017. "Coboat", accessed January, 2018. www.coboat.org/

Cobot. 2016. "Cobot - managing coworking spaces", accessed January, 2018. https://www.cobot.me/

Cobot. 2016. "Cobot Support Center". https://www.cobot.me/support#guides

Cohere Bandwidth. 2016. "Band Rehearsal Space", accessed January, 2016. https://coherebandwidth.com/

Cohere, LLC. 2016. "Cohere". http://coherecommunity.com/

CoPass. 2016. "CoPass", accessed January, 2018. https://copass.org/network

Cotivation. 2017
. "Cotivation - Collaborative motivation groups for coworking spaces", accessed January, 2018. http://cotivation.co/

Cottle, Frank. 2016. "A Foundation for Change: A single global voicex." Global Coworking Unconference Conference, Los Angeles, May 6. http://canada.gcuc.co/wp-

content/uploads/2016/presentations/Foundation%20and%20Giving
%20-%20Frank%20Cottle.pdf

Cowork Pass. 2016. "Cowork Pass", accessed January, 2016.
http://coworkunite.com/cowork-pass/

Coworking Africa. 2015. "Coworking Africa conference 2015", accessed
January, 2018. http://coworkingafrica.com/

Coworking Community Blog. 2011. *Coworking Community Blog.*
https://coworking.wordpress.com/

Coworking Discussion List. 2016. "Coworking Discussion List", accessed
January, 2018. https://groups.google.com/forum/#!forum/coworking

Coworking Europe. 2017. *Coworking Europe Blog.*
http://coworkingeurope.net/blog/

Coworking Europe. 2018. "Coworking Europe Conference", accessed
January 2018. http://coworkingeurope.net/

coworking.org. 2012. "Coworking Manifesto: The Future of Work",
accessed January, 2018. http://coworkingmanifesto.com/

Cropcho, James. 2016. "Coworking in NYC using Croissant." *New Worker
Magazine*, March 6 http://newworker.co/mag/coworking-in-nyc-
using-croissant/.

De Koven, Bernard. 2013. "The Coworking Connection." *Deep Fun with
Bernard De Koven*, August 5. http://www.deepfun.com/the-
coworking-connection/

De Solla Price, Derik J., and Donald Beaver. 1966. "Collaboration in an
Invisible College." *American Psychologist.* 21 (11):1011-1018

Delwiche, Aaron, and Jennifer Jacobs Henderson, eds. 2013. *The
Participatory Cultures Handbook*. New York: Routledge.

Deskmag. 2015. "The History of Coworking", accessed January, 2018.
http://www.tiki-toki.com/timeline/entry/156192/The-History-Of-
Coworking-Presented-By-Deskmag/#vars!date=1997-05-
04_03:19:52!

Deskmag. 2016. "about us." http://www.deskmag.com/en/about-us

Deskmag. 2016. "Deskmag: The Coworking Magazine", accessed January,
2018. http://www.deskmag.com/

Deskmag. 2017. The 2017 Global Coworking Survey. Accessed January,
2018. http://www.deskmag.com/en/background-of-the-2017-global-
coworking-survey

Deskmag. 2017. "The Global Coworking Survey." Global Coworking
Unconference Conferences (GCUC), New York, May
http://usa.gcuc.co/wp-content/uploads/2017/05/GCUC-2017-
Global-Coworking-Survey.pdf

Dictionary.com. 2016. "tummler", accessed January, 2018.
http://www.dictionary.com/browse/tummler

Disney, Jo. 2016. "NextKids Closure: Is There a Future for Coworking with Childcare?" *AllWork*, April 22. https://allwork.space/2016/04/nextkids-closure-is-there-a-future-for-coworking-with-childcare/

Doctorow, Cory. 2009. *Makers*. New York: Tor.

Duffett, Mark. 2013. *Understanding Fandom : An Introduction to the Study of Media Fan Culture*. New York: Bloomsbury.

Dunbar, R. I. M. 1992. "Neocortex size as a constraint on group size in primates." *Journal of Human Evolution* 22 (6):469-493. doi: 10.1016/0047-2484(92)90081-J. http://www.sciencedirect.com/science/article/pii/004724849290081J

Ebeling, Mick. 2015. *Not Impossible: The Art and Joy of Doing What Couldn't Be Done*. New York: Atria Books.

Emergent Research. 2016. "Emergent Research Tracking the Future of Small Business", accessed January, 2018. http://www.emergentresearch.com/

Florida, Richard. 2002. *The Rise of the Creative Class. And How It's Transforming Work, Leisure and Everyday Life*. New York: Basic Books.

Foertsch, Carsten. 2010. Why Coworkers like their Coworking Spaces. *Deskmag*. Accessed January, 2018. http://www.deskmag.com/en/why-coworkers-like-their-coworking-spaces-162

Foertsch, Carsten. 2011. First results of Global Coworking Survey. *Deskmag*. Accessed January, 2018. http://www.deskmag.com/en/first-results-of-global-coworking-survey-171

Foertsch, Carsten. 2012. 1st Results of the 3rd Global Coworking Survey. *Deskmag*. Accessed January, 2018. http://www.deskmag.com/en/1st-results-of-the-3rd-global-coworking-survey-2012

Foertsch, Carsten. 2014. The Coworking Forecast 2014. *Deskmag*. Accessed January, 2018. http://www.deskmag.com/en/the-coworking-market-report-forecast-2014

Foertsch, Carsten. 2015. First Results Of The New Global Coworking Survey. *Deskmag*. Accessed January, 2018. http://www.deskmag.com/en/first-results-of-the-new-global-coworking-survey-2015-16

Foertsch, Carsten. 2016. 2016 Global Coworking Survey. *Deskmag*. Accessed January, 2018. http://www.deskmag.com/en/2016-forecast-global-coworking-survey-results/2

Foertsch, Carsten. 2016. "Results of the Global Coworking Survey." Global
    Coworking Unconference Conference, Los Angeles, May 4.
    http://canada.gcuc.co/wp-
    content/uploads/2016/presentations/DESKMAG%20GCUC%20GL
    OBAL%20COWORKING%20SURVEY%20PRESENTATION%2
    02016%20SLIDES.pdf
Foertsch, Carsten. 2017. How profitable are coworking spaces today?
    Deskmag. Accessed January, 2018.
    http://www.deskmag.com/en/how-profitable-are-coworking-spaces-
    profitability-business-stats-statistics-make-money-965
Foertsch, Carsten. 2017. More than one million people will work in
    coworking spaces in 2017. *Deskmag*. Accessed January, 2018.
    http://www.deskmag.com/en/the-complete-2017-coworking-
    forecast-more-than-one-million-people-work-from-14000-
    coworking-spaces-s
Freelancers Union. 2015. Freelancing in America: 2015. New York:
    Freelancers Unioin and Upwork https://fu-web-storage-
    prod.s3.amazonaws.com/content/filer_public/59/e7/59e70be1-5730-
    4db8-919f-1d9b5024f939/survey_2015.pdf.
Freelancers Union. 2016. Freelancing in America: 2016. New York:
    Freelancers Union and Upwork https://fu-prod-
    storage.s3.amazonaws.com/content/None/FreelancinginAmerica201
    6report.pdf.
Freelancers Union. 2018. "The Freelancers Union", accessed January 2018.
    https://www.freelancersunion.org/
Freelancers Union, and UpWork. 2017. Freelancing in America: 2017.
    Freelancers Union https://s3.amazonaws.com/fuwt-prod-
    storage/content/FreelancingInAmericaReport-2017.pdf.
Fuzi, Anita, Nick Clifton, and Gareth H. Loudon. 2015. "New spaces for
    supporting entrepreneurship? Co-working spaces in the Welsh
    entrepreneurial landscape." 8th International Conference of
    entrepreneurship, innovation and regional development, , Sheffield,
    UK, June 18-19. http://hdl.handle.net/10369/7478
Gangplank Collective. 2016. "Manifesto - Gangplank", accessed January,
    2018. http://gangplankhq.com/vision/manifesto/
Garrett, Lyndon Earl, Gretchen M. Spreitzer, and Peter Bacevice. 2014.
    "Co-constructing a Sense of Community at Work: The Emergence
    of Community in Coworking Spaces." *Academy of Management
    Proceedings* 2014 (1). doi: 10.5465/ambpp.2014.139.
    http://proceedings.aom.org/content/2014/1/14004.abstract
Gerdenitsch, Cornelia, Tabea E Scheel, Julia Andorfer, and Christian
    Korunka. 2016. "Coworking Spaces: A Source of Social Support for

Independent Professionals." *Frontiers in psychology* 7:581.
https://www.ncbi.nlm.nih.gov/pmc/articles/PMC4843169/

Gershenfeld, Neil. 2005. *Fab: The Coming Revolution On Your Desktop-From Personal Computing to Personal Fabrication*. New York: Basic Books.

Glass, Anne P. 2012. Aging Better Together.   (2). Accessed January, 2018. http://www.secondjourney.org/itin/12_Sum/12Sum_Glass.htm

Global Coworking Unconference Conferences (GCUC) 2018. "Global Coworking Unconference Conferences (GCUC) ", accessed January, 2018. http://gcuc.co/

Greenfield, Susan. 2015. *Mind Change: How Digital Technologies Are Leaving Their Mark On Our Brains*. New York: Random House.

Grind. 2016. "Grind Coworking", accessed January, 2018. http://www.grindspaces.com/

Grusauskas, Maria. 2013. The Future of Coworking is Free and Augmented. http://www.shareable.net/blog/the-future-of-coworking-is-free-and-augmented

Hacker Lab. 2016. "Startup Coworking Space", accessed January, 2018. http://hackerlab.org/

Hamilton, Anita. 2014. The Public Library Wants To Be Your Office. Accessed January, 2018. http://www.fastcompany.com/3034143/the-public-library-wants-to-be-your-office

Happy Hubbub. 2017. "Happy Hubbub - coworking with children", accessed January, 2018. https://www.happyhubbub.com.au/

Hartmans, Avery. 2016. Here's why Microsoft is giving nearly a third of its New York employees memberships at WeWork. *Business Insider*. http://www.businessinsider.com/microsoft-new-york-workers-wework-2016-11

Hera Hub Headquarters. 2015. "Felena's inspiration for launching Hera Hub ". [YouTube Video]. Hera Hub Headquarters, accessed January, 2018. https://youtu.be/OTGP_T-AlQo

HeraHub. 2017. "Hera Hub: Workspace for Women", accessed January 2015. http://herahub.com/

Hillman, Alex. 2011. "Coworking Core Values 1 of 5: Sustainability", accessed January, 2018. http://dangerouslyawesome.com/2011/08/coworking-core-values-1-of-5-sustainability/

Hillman, Alex. 2011. "Coworking Core Values 2 of 5: Accessibility", accessed January, 2018. http://dangerouslyawesome.com/2011/08/coworking-core-values-2-of-5-accessibility/

Hillman, Alex. 2011. "Coworking Core Values 3 of 5: Openness", accessed January, 2018. http://dangerouslyawesome.com/2011/08/coworking-core-values-3-of-5-openness/

Hillman, Alex. 2011. "Coworking Core Values 4 of 5: Community", accessed January, 2018. http://dangerouslyawesome.com/2011/08/coworking-core-values-4-of-5-community/

Hillman, Alex. 2011. "Coworking Core Values 5 of 5: Collaboration", accessed January, 2018. http://dangerouslyawesome.com/2011/10/coworking-core-values-5-of-5-collaboration/

Hillman, Alex. 2013. "Indy Hall 2012: Reviewing Our Coworking Community by the Numbers." *Alex Hillman*, Feb 4. http://dangerouslyawesome.com/2013/02/indy-hall-2012-reviewing-our-coworking-community-by-the-numbers/

Hillman, Alex. 2014. "To build a strong community, stop "community managing", be a Tummler instead." *Alex Hillman*, April 20. http://dangerouslyawesome.com/2014/04/community-management-tummling-a-tale-of-two-mindsets/

Hillman, Alex. 2016. The problem with the coworking industry in 2016. *New Worker Magazine*. Accessed January, 2018. http://newworker.co/mag/the-problem-with-the-coworking-industry-in-2016/

Hindin, Michelle J. 2007. "Role Theory." In *Blackwell Encyclopedia of Sociology*, edited by George Ritzer, 2951-2954. Malden, MA: Blackwell Publishers.

Hoffice. 2017. "Hoffice: Come and work at someone's home", accessed January, 2018. http://hoffice.nu/en/

Hoffice. 2017. "Hosting & Facilitating", accessed January, 2018. http://hoffice.nu/en/hosting-facilitating/

Horowitz, Sara. 2012. *The Freelancer's Bible*. New York: Workman Publishing.

Hurry, Christopher J. P. 2012. "The Hub Halifax : a qualitative study on coworking." Masters of Business Administration Major Research Project, Business Administartion, St. Mary's University.

Icehouse. 2016. "Icehouse - Leasing office space in New Orleans", accessed January, 2018. http://www.icehousenola.com/

Impact Hub. 2016. "Impact Hub - Experience Collaborartion", accessed January, 2018. https://www.impacthub.net/

Impact Hub. 2016. "Impact Hub: Experience Collabortion", accessed January 2016. http://www.impacthub.net/

Independents Hall LLC. 2016. "Coworking in Philadelphia - Indy Hall - a Community and Workspace - Est. 2006", accessed January, 2018. http://www.indyhall.org/

Industrious. 2017. "Coworking Redefined", accessed January, 2018. https://www.industriousoffice.com/

Jacobs, Esther, and André Gussekloo. 2016. *Digital Nomads: How to Live, Work and Play Around the World*. Amazon.com: Self Published.

Jeffery, Al. 2016. Three Ways to Co-Create a Vibrant Co-living Culture. *Shareable*. Accessed January, 2018. http://www.shareable.net/blog/three-ways-to-co-create-a-vibrant-co-living-culture

Jelly. 2017. "Jelly: Working together is more fun for everyonw!", accessed January, 2018. http://workatjelly.com/

Johnson, Cat. 2015. 7 Essential Coworking Resources for Digital Nomads. *Shareable*. Accessed January, 2018. http://www.shareable.net/blog/7-essential-coworking-resources-for-digital-nomads

Johnson, Cat. 2015. Cotivation Helps Freelancers Succeed Through Mutual Accountability. *Shareable*. Accessed January, 2018. http://www.shareable.net/blog/cotivation-helps-freelancers-succeed-through-mutual-accountability

Johnson, Cat. 2015. The Top 10 Tips For Running a Coworking Space at Home. *Shareable*. Accessed January, 2018. http://www.shareable.net/blog/the-top-10-tips-for-running-a-coworking-space-at-home

Johnson, Cat. 2016. Aging in Community: Inside the Senior Cohousing Movement. *Shareable*. http://www.shareable.net/blog/aging-in-community-inside-the-senior-cohousing-movement

Johnson, Cat. 2016. Look Out, Coworking. Here Comes Big Money. *Shareable*. Accessed January, 2018. http://www.shareable.net/blog/look-out-coworking-here-comes-big-money

Johnson, Cat. 2016. Recap of the #FutureOfCoworking Twitter Chat. *Shareable*. Accessed January, 2018. http://www.shareable.net/blog/recap-of-the-futureofcoworking-twitter-chat

Johnson, Cat. 2017. 5 Coworking Spaces and Business Incubators in Libraries That Support Local Workers. *Shareable*. Accessed January, 2018. www.shareable.net/blog/5-coworking-spaces-and-business-incubators-in-libraries-that-support-local-workers

Jones, Drew, Todd Sundsted, and Tony Bacigalupo. 2009. *I'm Outta Here: How coworking is making the office obsolete*. Austin: Not an MBA Press.

Kane, Lori. 2012. "What is a friendship incubator?", accessed April, 2016. http://www.collectiveself.com/frequently-asked-questions/what-is-a-friendship-incubator/

Kane, Lori, Tabitha Borchardt, and Bas de Baar. 2015. *Reimagination Stations: Creating a Game-Changing In-Home Coworking Space*: Lori Kane.

Kavsen, Rhonda. 2016. "Co-Working Spaces Add a Perk for Parents: Child Care." *New York Times*, December 25, RE5, Style. http://www.nytimes.com/2016/12/23/realestate/co-working-spaces-add-a-perk-for-parents-child-care.html?_r=0.

Kennedy, Pagan. 2016. *Inventology: How We Dream Up Things That Change The World*. Boston: Houghton Miffin Harcourt.

King, Steve. 2011. Voices of Coworking. https://youtu.be/QtyTUNqc_Pk.

Klaas, Zachary R. 2014. Coworking & Connectivity in Berlin. University of Illinois at Urbana Champaign https://www.academia.edu/11486279/Coworking_Connectivity.

Kwiatkowski, Angel. 2011. "Coworking: An Easy Way To Green Your Business." *Cohere Community Blog*, May 9. http://coherecommunity.com/blog/coworking-green-your-business

Kwiatkowski, Angel. 2011. "Why Being Social Is More Important Than Social Media." *Cohere Community Blog*, February 23. http://coherecommunity.com/blog/being-social-is-more-important-than-social-media

Kwiatkowski, Angel, and Beth Buczynski. 2011. "Coworking: Building Community as a Space Catalyst." Ft. Collins: Cohere Coworking. http://coherecommunity.com/shop/coworking-building-community-as-a-space-catalyst (accessed January, 2018).

Kwiatkowski, Angel, and Beth Buczynski. 2011. "Coworking: How freelancers escape the coffee shop office and tales of community from independents around the world." Fort Collins: Cohere. http://coherecommunity.com/shop/coworkers (accessed January, 2018).

Link Coworking. 2017. "Link Coworking — Bringing People Together", accessed January, 2018. http://www.linkcoworking.com/

Liquid Talent. 2015. "Dude, Where's My Drone: The future of work and what you can do to prepare for it." https://www.dropbox.com/s/405kr9keucv97gw/LiquidTalentFoWEbook.pdf?dl=0 (accessed January, 2018).

LiquidSpace. 2017. "The LiquidSpace Network", accessed January, 2018. https://liquidspace.com/network-for-office-space

Lodgic Everyday Community. 2018. "Lodgic Everyday Community", accessed January, 2018. https://lodgic.org/

Luthera, Nader. 2016. Coworking our way around the world. *New Worker Magazine*. Accessed January, 2018. http://newworker.co/mag/cowork-the-world/

Lynn, Samara. 2016. "Finding the Perfect Co-working Space." *Black Enterprise* 46 (9):58-59

Maggs, Sam. 2015. *The Fangirl's Guide to the Galaxy: a Handbook for Geek Girls*. Philadelphia: Quirk Books.

Make Shift Boston. 2016. "Make Shift Boston", accessed January, 2018. http://makeshiftboston.org/space

Manning, Peter Kirby. 2007. "Dramaturgy." In *Blackwell Encyclopedia of Sociology*, edited by George Ritzer, 1226-1229. Malden, MA: Blackwell Publishers.

Marshall, Claire. 2015. "How to Make Money (and a whole lot more) by Sharing." Self Published. https://www.sharestories.net/the-book (accessed January, 2018).

Marshall, Fraser A., and Justin M. Witman. 2010. "Humantics: The Science and Design of Sustainable Collaboration." Master of Industrial Design Industrial Design Program, The University of the Arts

Martin, Courtney E. 2016. *The New Better Off: Reinventing the American Dream*. Berkeley: Seal Press.

Matrix Coworking. 2017. "Matrix Coworking", accessed January, 2018. http://www.matrixcbsolutions.com/en

McConnon, Aili. 2017. "Starting Up a Business, With Little Ones Close By." *New York Times*, April 20. https://www.nytimes.com/2017/04/19/business/smallbusiness/coworking-spaces-daycare-child-care-entrepreneurs.html.

McGonigal, Jane. 2015. *Superbetter: A Revolutionary Approach to Getting Stronger, Happier, Braver, and More Resilient*. New York: Penguin Press.

McGrath, Robert. 2014. "You Shall Not Crucify The Internet On This Cross of Bitcoin." *Very Much Wow*, July, 34-37 http://issuu.com/verymuchwow/docs/vmw3/35?e=11558635/8421855.

McLaren, Diana. 2015. Australian Coworking Event a Window into Growing Movement. *Shareable*. Accessed January, 2018. http://www.shareable.net/blog/australian-coworking-event-a-window-into-growing-movement

Meetup. 2017. "Find Your People - Meetup", accessed January, 2018.
https://www.meetup.com/

Merkel, Janet. 2015. "Coworking in the city." *Ephemera* 15 (1):121

Mesku, Melissa. 2015. Coworking: the best place for hookups in 2015? *The New Worker*. Accessed January, 2018.
http://newworker.co/mag/coworking-dating-hookup/

Mesku, Melissa. 2016. Community: the key thing. *New Worker Magazine*. Accessed January, 2018. http://newworker.co/mag/what-your-key-says-about-your-coworking-space/

Mesku, Melissa. 2016. Quantifying serendipity. *New Worker Magazine*. Accessed January, 2018. http://newworker.co/mag/quantifying-serendipity-in-coworking/

Miller, Anna Bergren. 2014. Enspiral: Changing the Way Social Entrepreneurs Do Business. *Sharable*. Accessed January, 2018. http://www.shareable.net/blog/enspiral-changing-the-way-social-entrepreneurs-do-business

Miritello, Giovanna, Esteban Moro, Rubén Lara, Rocío Martínez-López, Sam G. B. Roberts, and Robin I. M. Dunbar. 2013. Time as a Limited Resource: Communication Strategy in Mobile Phone Networks. arXiv https://arxiv.org/abs/1301.2464.

Mok, Kimberley. 2016. "Can co-working vacations offer a better work-life balance?" *Treehuggger*, September 22. http://www.treehugger.com/culture/coworkations-better-work-life-balance.html

Nebula. 2017. "Nebula Coworking St. Louis", accessed January, 2018. https://nebulastl.com/

Neuberg, Brad. 2014. "The Start of Coworking (from the Guy that Started It)." *coding in paradise*, January 16. http://codinginparadise.org/ebooks/html/blog/start_of_coworking.html

New Worker Magazine. 2016. About. Accessed January, 2018. http://newworker.co/mag/about/

NextSpace. 2016. "NextSpace", accessed January, 2016. http://nextspace.us/

NextSpace. 2016. "We're Hiring Community Builders", accessed March, 2016. http://nextspace.us/2016/02/22/were-hiring-sf/

NextSpace. 2017. "Careers At NextSpace", accessed March, 2016. http://nextspace.us/careers

Nexudus. 2017. "Nexudus: The white-label coworking software", accessed January, 2018. http://coworking.nexudus.com/en

Nomad House. 2018. "Nomad House - Start your online business while exploring some of the most beautiful places", accessed January, 2018. https://nomadhouse.io/

Office Nomads. 2016. "Office Nomads", accessed January, 2018.
http://officenomads.com/

Office Nomads. 2017. "The Nadine Project", accessed January, 2018.
http://nadineproject.org/

OfficeR&D. 2018. "Coworking Directories", accessed January.
https://officernd.com/list-of-coworking-directories/

Olma, Sebastian. 2012. "The Serendipity Machine: A Disruptive Business
Model for Society 3.0."
https://www.seats2meet.com/downloads/The_Serendipity_Machine.
pdf (accessed January 2018).

One Roof. 2017. "One Roof", accessed January,
2018.]http://www.oneroofwomen.com/

Open Coworking. 2016. "Open Coworking - Building the movement
together", accessed January, 2018. http://opencoworking.org/

Our Enspiral Spaces. 2015. "Enspiral Space", accessed January, 2015.
https://enspiral.com/our-spaces/

Oxford International Institute. 2016. "Introducing the iLabour Project",
accessed January, 2018. http://ilabour.oii.ox.ac.uk/

Paragraph. 2016. "Paragraph: Workspace for Writers", accessed January,
2018. http://www.paragraphny.com/

Phoenix Public Library. 2016. "About hive", accessed January, 2018.
https://www.phoenixpubliclibrary.org/hive/Pages/About-hive.aspx

Piketty, Thomas. 2014. *Capital in the Twenty-First Century*. Translated by
Arthur Goldhammer. Cambridge, MA: Harvard University Press.

Popper, Nathaniel. 2015. *Digital Gold: Bitcoin And The Inside Story of The
Misfits and Millionaires Trying to Reinvent Money*. New York:
HarperCollins.

Portland Engine Room. 2016. "Space - Engine room", accessed January,
2018. http://portlandengineroom.com/space/

Projective. 2016. "Projective", accessed January, 2018.
http://www.projective.co/

Proximity Space. 2017. "Connecting Communities & Coworking Spaces",
accessed January, 2018. https://proximity.space/

Rail Yard. 2016. "Rail Yard", accessed January, 2018.
http://www.railyardtucson.com/#the-space

Renascent Hospitality LLC. 2016. "Serendipity Labs Coworking Coming to
Columbus", accessed January, 2018.
http://www.renascenthospitality.com/Blog/174748/Serendipity-
Labs-Coworking-Coming-to-Columbus

Ritzer, George, ed. 2007. *The Blackwell Encyclopedia of Sociology*. Malden,
MA: Blackwell.

Salinsky, Tom, and Deborah Frances-White. 2008. *The Improv Handbook: The Ultimate Guide to Improvising in Comedy, Theater, and Beyond*. New York: Teh continuum International Publicshing Group, Inc.

Scholz, Trebor. 2016. Platform Cooperativism: Challenging the Corporate Sharing Economy. New York: Rosa Luxemburg Stiftung: New York Office http://www.rosalux-nyc.org/platform-cooperativism-2/.

Seats2Meet. 2016. "Our Locations", accessed January, 2018. https://www.seats2meet.com/en/locations

Seats2Meet. 2016. "Seats2Meet - Connecting and empowering you to excel", accessed January, 2018. https://www.seats2meet.com/en

Seattle Collaborative Space Alliance. 2016. "Seattle Collaborative Space Alliance (SCSA)", accessed January, 2018. http://collaborativespaces.org/

Sheridan, Richard. 2013. *Joy, Inc.: How We Built a Workplace People Love*. New York: Penguin.

Shermer, Michael. 2014. "Surviving Statistics." *Scientific American* 311 (3):94-94. https://www.scientificamerican.com/article/how-the-survivor-bias-distorts-reality/

Shirky, Clay. 2010. *Cognitive Surplus: Creativity and Generosity in a Connected Age*. New York: The Penguin Press.

SLO Makerspace. 2016. "Cubicles - SLO Makerspace", accessed January, 2018. http://www.slomakerspace.com/cubicles/

Smith, Gary. 2014. *Standard Deviations: Flawed Assumptions, Tortured Data, and Other Ways to Lie With Statistics* New York: Overlook Duckworth.

Spark Labs. 2016. "Welcome: Spark Labs", accessed January, 2016. http://www.spark-labs.co/en

Spinuzzi, Clay. 2012. "Working Alone Together: Coworking as Emergent Collaborative Activity." *Journal of Business and Technical Communication* 26 (4):399-441. doi: 10.1177/1050651912444070. http://jbt.sagepub.com/content/26/4/399.abstract

Spolin, Viola. 1999. *Improvisation for the Theater: A Handbook of Teaching and Directing Techniques (Third Edition)*. Evanston: Northwestern University Press.

Spreitzer, Gretchen, Peter Bacevice, and Lyndon Garrett. 2015. "Why People Thrive in Coworking Spaces." *Harvard Business Review* 93 (8):1-7. https://hbr.org/2015/05/why-people-thrive-in-coworking-spaces

Stark, Kevin. 2017. Oxford Internet Institute Launches Interactive Map of the Global Gig Economy. *Shareable*. Accessed January, 2018.

http://www.shareable.net/blog/oxford-internet-institute-launches-interactive-map-of-the-global-gig-economy

Steve. 2015. "Coworking Spaces are Human Spaces." *Small Business Labs*, May 12. http://www.smallbizlabs.com/2015/05/coworking-spaces-are-human-spaces.html

Strongbox West. 2015. "Strongbox West ", accessed January, 2018. http://www.strongboxwest.com/

Sub Urban Co-Working. 2017. "Sub Urban Co-Working", accessed January, 2018. http://www.suburban.org.nz/

Sundesk. 2016. "Sundesk: Coworking in Taghazout, Morocco", accessed January, 2016. http://www.sun-desk.com/

Sunstein, Cass R. 2006. *Infotopia: How Many Minds Produce Knowledge*. New York: Oxford University Press.

Surman, Tonya. 2013. "Building Social Entrepreneurship through the Power of Coworking." *Innovations: Technology, Governance, Globalization* 8 (3-4):189-195. doi: 10.1162/INOV_a_00195. http://dx.doi.org/10.1162/INOV_a_00195

Tapscott, Don, and Anthony D. Williams. 2006. *Wikinomics: How Mass Collaboration Changes Everything*. New York: Penguin.

The Center for Positive Organizations. 2016. "University of Michigan Coworking Project", accessed May, 2016. https://ctools.umich.edu/access/content/group/26e1cf0a-9db8-45cb-9a22-92365294579f/index.html

The Centre for Social Innovation. 2016. "Culture | The Centre for Social Innovation", accessed January, 2018. https://socialinnovation.org/culture/

The Centre for Social Innovation. 2016. Emergence: The Story of The Centre for Social Innovation. http://socialinnovation.ca/sites/socialinnovation.ca/files/Emergence_The_Story_of_the_Centre_for_Social_Innovation.pdf.

The Centre for Social Innovation. 2016. Proof: How Shared Spaces are Changing the World. http://socialinnovation.ca/sites/socialinnovation.ca/files/Proof_How_shared_spaces_are_changing_the_world_.pdf.

The Centre for Social Innovation. 2016. Rigour: How-To Create World-Changing Spaces. http://socialinnovation.ca/sites/socialinnovation.ca/files/Rigour_How_to_create_World-Changing_Shared_Spaces_.pdf.

The CoWorking Institute. 2015. "The CoWorking Institute", accessed January, 2016. http://coworking.net/

The Coworking Pass Europe. 2016. "The Coworking Pass Europe",
    accessed January, 2016.
    http://www.lespotmultiburo.com/coworking-pass-en/
The Coworking Wiki. 2015. "Coworking Manifesto (global - for the world)
    " *The Coworking Wiki*.
    http://wiki.coworking.org/w/page/35382594/Coworking%20Manife
    sto%20%28global%20-%20for%20the%20world%29
The Coworking Wiki. 2015. "Coworking Space Directory", accessed
    January, 2018.
    http://wiki.coworking.org/w/page/29303049/Directory
The Coworking Wiki. 2015. "The Values of Open Coworking", accessed
    January, 2018.
    http://wiki.coworking.org/w/page/67817489/The%20Values%20of
    %20Open%20Coworking
The Coworking Wiki. 2016. "The Coworking Wiki", accessed January,
    2018. http://wiki.coworking.org/w/page/16583831/FrontPage
The Global Coworking Blog. 2015. *The Global Coworking Blog*.
    http://blog.coworking.com/
The Harlem Collective. 2017. "The Harlem Collective", accessed January,
    2018. http://www.theharlemcollective.co/
The Hatchery Press. 2016. "The Hatchery Press - Where Stories Are Born",
    accessed January, 2018. http://thehatcherypress.com/
The Indy Hall Braintrust. 2017. "The club for professional community
    builders ", accessed January, 2018.
    https://theindyhallway.com/braintrust/
The League of Extraordinary Coworking Spaces. 2016. "The League of
    Extraordinary Coworking Spaces", accessed January, 2018.
    http://lexc.org/
The Left Bank Project. 2016. "Hive at the Left Bank", accessed January,
    2018. http://leftbankproject.com/hive/
The Makers Space. 2016. "The Makers Space - Seattle", accessed January,
    2018. http://www.themakersspace.com/
The Shift. 2017. "The Shift - Home", accessed January, 2018.
    http://www.theshiftchicago.com/
The Surf Office. 2015. "The Surf Office Santa Cruz", accessed January,
    2018. http://www.thesurfoffice.com/santa-cruz/
The Wing. 2017. "The Wing", accessed January, 2018. https://www.the-
    wing.com/
TheCo. 2016. "Coworking Maker Space", accessed January, 2018.
    http://www.attheco.com/
theOffice. 2016. "theOffice - where creativity takes flight", accessed
    January, 2018. http://theofficeonline.com/

Think Big Coworking. 2017. "Think Big Coworking", accessed January, 2018. http://thinkbigcoworking.com/

Thompson, Claire. 2012. Cohousing: The Secret to Sustainable Urban Living? *Grist*. Accessed January, 2018. http://grist.org/cities/cohousing-the-secret-to-sustainable-urban-living/

Thrive. 2017. "Welcome Home", accessed January, 2018. https://www.thriveaz.com/

Turkle, Sherry. 2015. *Reclaiming Conversation: The Power of Talk in a Digital Age*. New York: Penguin Press.

University of Illinois. 2017. "Enterpriseworks Affiliates Program - Research Park", accessed January, 2018. http://www.researchpark.illinois.edu/resources/enterpriseworks-affiliate-program

Van de Vrande, Vareska, and Michiel Tempelaar. 2015. Creating Communities of Innovation. Rotterdam: Rotterdam School of Management, Erasmus University http://api.rsm.nl/files/index/get/id/1aabed80-8ebb-11e5-8275-c1f4f8ce46f7.

Wetstein, Jonathan P. 2010. Leadership Practices of Indy Hall's Coworking Initiative. Philadelphia: The University of the Arts Master of Industrial Design Program https://dl.dropboxusercontent.com/u/628073/IHResearch/Wetstein_IndyHall_Research.pdf.

WeWork. 2015. "WeWork: Create Your Life's Work", accessed January, 2018. https://www.wework.com/

Widdicombe, Lizzie. 2016. "Happy together." *The New Yorker*, May 16, 48-55.

Wikipedia. 2016. "Open-source model", accessed January, 2018. https://en.wikipedia.org/wiki/Open-source_model

Wikipedia. 2017. "Ship of Theseus", accessed January, 2018. https://en.wikipedia.org/wiki/Ship_of_Theseus

Wikipedia. 2018. "Coworking", accessed January, 2018. https://en.wikipedia.org/wiki/Coworking

Wolf, Andeas. 2016. How to "Hoffice" with Other Freelancers for More Health, Happiness and Productivity. *Sharable*. Accessed January, 2018. http://www.shareable.net/blog/how-to-hoffice-with-other-freelancers-for-more-health-happiness-and-productivity

Women's Business Incubator. 2016. "Women's Business Incubator", accessed March 18, 2016. http://womensincubator.org/

Work and Play. 2016. "Work and Play", accessed January, 2018. http://www.workandplaynj.com/

Zoref, Lior. 2015. *Mindsharing: The Art of Crowdsourcing Everything.* New York: Penguin.

www.ingramcontent.com/pod-product-compliance
Lightning Source LLC
Chambersburg PA
CBHW032006170526
45157CB00002B/570